Heaven on Your Head

INTERPRETATIONS, LEGENDS AND PARABLES
COMMENTS ON THE TORAH AND THE HOLIDAYS

As narrated by RABBI S. Z. KAHANA
Director of the Ministry of Religious Affairs
State of Israel

Edited and Adapted by
RABBI MORRIS SILVERMAN

Illustrations by Meir Ben-Uri

RESEARCH CENTRE OF KABBALAH
JERUSALEM – NEW YORK

©

Copyright by the Author

Research Centre Book of Related Interest
Ask your bookseller for the books you have missed

ENTRANCE TO THE ZOHAR, compiled and edited by Dr. Philip S. Berg
ENTRANCE TO THE TREE OF LIFE, compiled and edited by Dr. Philip S. Berg
KABBALAH FOR THE LAYMAN, by Dr. Philip S. Berg
TEN LUMINOUS EMANATIONS, vol. 1, compiled and edited by R. Levi Krakovsky
TEN LUMINOUS EMANATIONS, vol. 2, compiled and edited by Dr. Philip S. Berg
LIGHT OF REDEMPTION, by Levi Krakovsky
GENERAL PRINCIPLES OF KABBALAH, by R. Moses H. Luzatto
REINCARNATION: THE WHEELS OF A SOUL, by Dr. Philip S. Berg
KABBALAH: A GIFT OF THE BIBLE, by R. Yehuda Ashlag
POWER OF THE ALEPH BETH, by Dr. Philip S. Berg
ASTROLOGY: AN ECHO OF THE FUTURE, by Dr. Philip S. Berg

BOOK IN PRINT

KABBALISTIC MEDITATION, by Dr. Philip S. Berg

Printed in the United States of America

1986

PREFACE

On my fifth visit to Israel, I had the good fortune to meet Dr. Shmuel Zanvil Kahana, whose erudition and originality this book attempts to reflect. I was deeply impressed by his seminal mind, his mystical insights, and his extraordinary capacity to elucidate profound truths through metaphors, parables and analogies. Dr. Kahana's talks invariably revealed his scholarship and a concern for the human situation in the world today; and his fertile ideas were couched in the language of ancient texts. His discourses are tantamount to a revival of a classical Jewish genre: the tradition of teaching through legend.

Dr. Kahana is descended from a distinguished line of Rabbis and preachers. His father, Shlomo David, was for many years before settling in Jerusalem, the Chief Rabbi of Warsaw. A many-faceted personality, Rabbi Shmuel Zanvil Kahana holds an important administrative position in the Government of Israel as Director of the Ministry of Religious Affairs. Among his several responsibilities is that of Curator of Mount Zion, one of Israel's sacred sites. He is also Rabbi of the well-known Bilu Synagogue and school in Tel Aviv.

After writing a number of serious works on philosophy, including a study on Maimonides, Dr. Kahana turned his attention to mysticism and to the *Aggadah*. He collected thousands of old legends and created many original *Aggadot* pertaining to the Bible, the Holy Days and Festivals. An enchanting raconteur, he might be considered the Israeli Hans Christian Andersen. His is the conviction that, whereas the *Halakha* (the legal aspects of Judaism) brings heaven to its students, the *Aggadah* (the legends and parables) transports them to heaven.

Dr. Kahana is the author of the following books published in Israel: *Menorat Hahar* (The Lamp of the Mountain), *Horshat Hahar* (The Grove on the Mountain), *Aggadot Dehathalta* (Legends of the Rebirth), *Bemirtzefet Hamazalot* (In the Path of the Zodiac) and *Begilgulay Hashanah* (The Cycle of the Year).

I feel certain that Rabbi Kahana's intuitive discernment, particularly in those portions of this book relating to the Bible and the Holidays, will not only interest teachers of all faiths, but will enlighten all lovers of the Bible and those who appreciate this specific method of Biblical Commentary which continues even in our own day.

When I discussed with Rabbi Kahana the value of having his interpretations made available in English in order to reach a wider public, he agreed, provided that I undertake this task. I gladly consented and, during my four months' sojourn in Israel, we met repeatedly in order that I might hear and record his notes and observations on the Five Books of Moses and the Holidays.

If it is difficult at best to translate faithfully a manuscript from one language into another and retain the style, substance and flavor of the original, how much more so to reconstruct and interpret these comments from notes, and then modify, amplify, and occasionally introduce other illustrations in order to bring out Dr. Kahana's ideas and render them more adaptable for English readers.

HEAVEN ON YOUR HEAD contains several comments on each of the fifty-four weekly portions of the Five Books of Moses, and on each of the Holy Days and Festivals.

The ornamental titles and drawings were especially designed for this volume by the Israeli artist, Meir Ben-Uri of Haifa.

I hope that this presentation of Rabbi Kahana's "Oral Torah" will, through the ancient medium of *Aggadah,* effectively convey to English readers of all faiths, his delightful legends, incisive comments and mystical insights.

Morris Silverman

CONTENTS

Comments on the Torah (The Five Books of Moses)

Comments on the Holy Days and Festivals

ILLUSTRATIONS

ABOUT THE ARTIST . . .

Meir Ben-Uri was born Maximilian Wasbutsky in Riga, Latvia, in 1909.

He studied in Berlin and graduated as engineer and architect. Under the influence of Rabbi Emil Nathan Levi, he became an observant orthodox Jew, Hebraized his name to Ben-Uri and in 1934 went to Israel and settled in Haifa.

As a disciple of Herman Struck, Ben-Uri devoted his talents to etching and painting.

As a town planner, Ben-Uri drew up the designs of Kfar Hanoar Hadati, Tirat Zvi, Sde Eliyahu, Kfar Etzion, and Ein Tzurim. He also designed the imposing buildings of Yeshiva Kerem B'Yavne and Yeshiva Haklait at Kfar Haroch (Yeshivath Bnai Akiva).

In addition to painting and architecture, Mr. Ben-Uri is also an accomplished musician and composed numerous works on Biblical themes as well as modern Israeli songs.

Mr. Ben-Uri serves as Architectural Adviser to the Ministry of Religion, and is Director of the Studio for Synagogal Arts in Kiryat Shmuel, Haifa.

בְּרֵאשִׁית

One of the most striking episodes in the Book of Genesis is Jacob's dream on a mountain in Jerusalem, the Holy City. Lying asleep, Jacob, later renamed Israel, is disturbed by a dream. He sees angels climbing first up and then down a ladder between heaven and earth. These wingless angels symbolize not only the sons of Jacob, but Moses, Aaron, Joshua, David, Solomon, the Prophets, the venerable Rabbis, the spiritual and political leaders of the Jewish people, the heroes of Jewish history from ancient times to the present redemption.

The top of the ladder is out of sight in the heavens. Around the foot of the ladder, dark, winged, diabolical creatures are trying to obstruct the ascent from earth to heaven and delay Israel's approach to God. But despite all obstacles, Jacob is determined to ascend the ladder.

And he dreamed . . . . . . וַיַּחֲלֹם וְהִנֵּה

and behold a ladder . . . . סֻלָּם

set up on the earth . . . . מֻצָּב אַרְצָה

28:12   כ"ח י"ב

GENESIS

HEAVEN ON YOUR HEAD

In the beginning God created the heaven and the earth
(Genesis 1:1).

There is a story told that in the early stages of creation, Heaven and Earth whirled in space like two huge spheres. Beholding this wonder, all the angels were filled with awe and sought shelter under the protecting arms of the Lord. But two of the angels, although spellbound by the spectacle, were unafraid and asked the Lord if they might have these spheres as their own.

At first the Lord was reluctant. How could He give away Heaven and Earth? But on reconsideration, He said to one of the angels: "I shall grant your request and give you Earth." Jubilant, the angel took Earth and gleefully bounced it back and forth.

Then the Lord said to the second angel: "Michael, to you I give Heaven." Overjoyed, Michael took Heaven and, because it was soft and vaulted, tenderly placed it like a cap upon his head.

After many centuries, the angel to whom Earth was given, grew tired of bouncing it and gave it to a giant who placed it upon his shoulders. Bearing the weight of the whole world, this giant settled on an island in the Mediterranean and proclaimed: "I am Atlas, Master of Crete!"

But the angel Michael, still wearing Heaven like a cap upon his head, settled in Jerusalem and became the guardian angel of the Children of Israel. Ever since then every Israelite, like Michael, has accepted Heaven as his possession.

And this, the story relates, is the origin of the *kippah* "skullcap" or *yarmulke*. It is to remind its wearer that, while others may carry Earth on their shoulders, the Jew is to carry Heaven on his head and work with his fellow men to bring the Kingdom of Heaven here on earth.

THE FUTILITY OF "IF"

*Eve also gave of the fruit to her husband (Adam) and he ate
(Genesis 3:6).*

A disciple said to the sage Elimelekh: "According to Kabalistic lore, the souls of all men were incorporated in Adam. If
this is so, then you were part of him when he accepted the apple
from Eve. You saw that he was about to sin. Why did you not
prevent him?"

"I could have prevented Adam from eating the apple," replied Elimelekh, "but if I had, he would have resented it all
his life. He would always have thought: 'If only I had eaten
from the apple, I might have been like God.' I refrained from
stopping him because I did not want him to have any regrets,
lest he spend his life brooding over what might have been, and
complaining: 'if—if—I had only done this.'

"Man frequently broods over missed opportunities, but it is
futile to worry about what might have been. The current situation is the only reality. The here and now is all we have. We
serve God here and now or not at all."

ENOCH'S SHOES

Enoch walked with God; then he was no more, for God took him (Genesis 5:24).

In our ancient literature we are told that Enoch is one of the nine men who live forever. Like the Prophet Elijah, he did not die but was carried up to heaven. When Enoch arrived in heaven, an angel met him and inquired: "How do you prefer to occupy yourself here in heaven?"

"I would like to make shoes," replied Enoch.

Astonished, the angel asked him why he wanted to make shoes.

Enoch explained: "When God drove out my great-great-great grandfather, Adam, from the Garden of Eden, Adam tried to return, but for a long time could not find the way. When he finally found the path it was infested with serpents. The serpent who had caused Adam to be expelled from the Garden was determined to prevent him from returning, and sent all these other snakes to terrify him and keep him away. These serpents were ready to strike and Adam was forced to turn back; therefore, I want to make shoes which will protect those who wear them so that all who seek the Garden of Eden may be able to enter."

Mystics believe that the victims of Europe's concentration camps who have survived the horrible holocaust were wearing the shoes which Enoch made when they escaped the brutalities of the Nazis and found their Garden of Eden in the State of Israel where they now live in dignity, joy and freedom.

EXAGGERATED VIRTUES

. . . Noah was in his generation a righteous man without blemish; Noah walked with God (Genesis 6:9).

Commenting on the phrase: "In his generation," the Rabbis give two interpretations. One holds that it is in praise of Noah because he was righteous even in a wicked generation. The other regards it as a criticism of Noah; he was righteous in comparison with the people in his generation but, had he lived in the days of Abraham, he would not have been considered righteous at all.

There is a Hasidic tale that a cemetery caretaker once reported he had heard in the night the sound of hammering on a tombstone. Nobody believed him. The next night several people went with the caretaker to the cemetery and heard the same sound. They called the Hasidic Rabbi and, with lighted candles accompanied him to a grave where they found their deceased friend Baruch busily engaged with his hammer and chisel pounding away on his own tombstone.

"Baruch!" the people cried out. "We buried you last week! What are you doing here?"

Baruch looked up at them with hollow, lifeless eyes. "When I reached heaven," he said, "the angels asked me who I was and what I did on earth. I informed them they could get the information from the epitaph which my dear ones had inscribed on my tombstone. On it the angels read: *Reb Baruch yoray shamayim, yodea sefer, ubaal tzdakah* 'Reb Baruch, the pious man, the learned Jew, the charitable person.'

"The angels then led me to the section occupied by the God-fearing men and found that I did not qualify. So they brought me to the scholars' section and found that I lacked learning.

Finally, they took me to those who had done much charity on earth and found that my contributions had been niggardly. It was thereupon decided that I must go down to the cemetery and obliterate that inscription because my virtues had been exaggerated by those who loved me. So here I am."

"Ah," declared the Rabbi, "I understand. The same is true of Noah. In the Bible we read: 'Noah was in his generation a righteous man without blemish; Noah walked with God.' But later, in Chapters 8 and 9, Noah's name is mentioned without the adjective 'righteous'; undoubtedly because he had disgraced himself when he became intoxicated after leaving the ark."

Baruch put down his hammer and chisel. "You see," he said. "Even Noah's epitaph had to be changed. My friends," he chuckled, "you'll find that many tombstones will have to be corrected when it is discovered in heaven that dear ones have exaggerated the virtues of their departed."

THE NEW ARK

*God said to Noah: "I have decided to put an end to all flesh,
for the earth is filled with violence because of them; I am about
to destroy them with the earth. Make for yourself an ark . . ."*
(Genesis 6:13,14).

Several years ago a team of American archaeologists traveled
to the Near East in an unsuccessful search of the remains of
Noah's ark. Arriving in Jerusalem in the hope of finding some
clues, they were advised to consult the Curator of Mount Zion,
who is an eminent student of antiquities and of ancient lore, and
an expert on the sacred sites in the Holy Land. When they were
introduced to him and told him their mission, he said: "I am
ready to show you the ark of Noah."

They were skeptical but there was something about the
Curator's manner which convinced them that he was in earnest.
When he said he would take them on a three days' journey,
they agreed to follow him. He imposed one condition: they
must ask no questions until after the expedition.

They assented and, on the following day, set out with him for
the Galil, in northern Israel. There they came to a village in
which many immigrants were building houses. The place was
a beehive of activity; some were sawing lumber; others were
hammering and putting in two-by-fours. By twilight the frames
of hundreds of buildings had been erected. The archaeologists
learned from the workers that on the previous day a ship had
brought them from Rumania and Hungary. There they had
been oppressed as outcasts; here, welcomed as free men, they
were already building new homes.

The next day the Curator conducted the archaeologists further into the Negev desert in the south of Israel. Here again they
saw the same sight. Hundreds of Jews, having just arrived by
ship from Morocco and other countries where they had been
persecuted, were now joyfully erecting new homes. In a single
day a whole settlement had arisen.

The third day the Curator brought the archaeologists to the outskirts of Jerusalem where they witnessed similar activities. At long last he explained:

"The story of the ark is not merely an episode that happened centuries ago in the days of Noah; in our time it is being re-enacted day after day. From many countries, immigrants threatened with annihilation by the inundation of inhumanity in the twentieth century, are today building their new ark in Israel. Why look for the remains of Noah's ark? Here in Israel is a new ark, and this historic event may well be regarded as the sequel to the Biblical account of Noah's ark. "Even as the ark saved Noah and his family from the Flood, these immigrants who are building a new society based on the social ideals of the Prophets of old, may in our own time be constructing the new ark that will salvage humanity."

THE ARK OF OUR LIVES

Make for yourselves an ark . . . (Genesis 6:14).

The incidents in the Bible are of interest not only because they tell of events that have happened but because they foreshadow events that will again occur. There will be floods and world catastrophes, and there will also be righteous men like Noah. But what does the ark represent?

The ark has a dual symbolism. It is not only a boat in which humanity can find shelter, ride through the storm and survive; it is also the repository of the Torah. The receptacle in which the Torah is kept is called the Holy Ark. And it is our task to convert the entire world into an Ark for the Torah whose teachings, if obeyed and followed, shall keep our generation safe from all danger. It was through Noah's ark that the world in his day was saved, and in our day the Ark of the Torah can also save the world.

Noah spent 120 years, the proverbial span of a lifetime, in building his ark. This teaches us that, as long as he lives, man should occupy himself with building his Ark—the Ark of his life. Only if our life becomes an Ark for the Torah shall we be safe from the dangers that threaten to overwhelm and engulf us.

The Ark in itself is merely a cabinet of wood; only when the Torah is placed in it does it become sacred. Thus it is with our life. The human body is only a physical vessel but when we fill it with holiness it becomes a Holy Ark.

The world is threatened by a Flood of destruction; therefore, in order to save humanity, it is essential that our world leaders build that Ark which shall contain the precepts of justice and peace taught in the Bible.

FALSEHOOD AND TRUTH

Of everything that creeps on the ground, two of each creature, male and female, came to Noah into the ark . . . (Genesis 7:8,9).

This verse tells us that no living creature could gain admittance into the ark if he were without a mate.

The story is told that Falsehood, desiring to enter the ark, was in search of a companion. Seeing Truth on his way to the ark, Falsehood decided to join him and said: "Let's go in together. You are known because of me; therefore I am a suitable companion for you." Truth consented but, as they approached the ark, Falsehood became apprehensive lest Noah refuse to admit him; he asked Truth to lend him his cloak so that he would not be recognized.

"You don't need a cloak," said Falsehood, "because everyone will instantly recognize you as Truth."

Truth agreed, and both were admitted into the ark. After the Flood, Falsehood left the ark without returning his companion's cloak. And ever since, Falsehood has been wearing the cloak of Truth. This is why it is often difficult to recognize Falsehood. As Shakespeare put it: "Oh, what a goodly outside Falsehood hath!"

In the same way, War and Peace must also have entered Noah's ark. Certainly War has garbed itself in the garments of Peace and many leaders, while planning war, pose as the advocates of peace. History is replete with examples of those who have talked peace but made war. People everywhere are thus confused. If we are not to be deceived into following the wrong leaders, we must learn to distinguish the genuine from the false, the real from the illusory.

HOW GREAT IS THE PERFORMANCE
OF A MITZVAH!

. . . Go forth from your native land and from your father's house to the land that I will show you (Genesis 12:1).

Rabbi Nahum of Chernoble devoted his entire life to the *mitzvah* (religious imperative) of *pidyon shevuyim* "the rescue of captives and imprisoned." One day, on a false charge, the Czar's officers threw the Rabbi himself into prison. It is said that his disciples, shocked, complained to God:

"Here is a man who has devoted his entire life to saving others from prison. How could You, O God, allow *him* to be thrust into prison?"

And God replied: "All his life Abraham fulfilled the *mitzvah* of *hakhnosat orhim* 'hospitality to the stranger and wayfarer.' His tent was always open to the stranger for whom he invariably provided food and shelter. Yet I bade him to go forth from his native land and from his father's house to the land which I would show him. Thus, he himself became a wayfarer in a strange land. And why did I do this? So that Abraham might realize how great is the *mitzvah* of befriending a wayfarer and a stranger.

"Likewise Rabbi Nahum, who had rescued so many, now himself a prisoner, fully appreciates how great is the *mitzvah* of rescuing captives and those who are imprisoned."

TO WHOM DOES THE LAND BELONG?

And the Lord said to Abram . . . : "Raise your eyes and look out from where you are, to the north and south, to the east and west, for I give all the land that you see, to you and your offspring forever" (Genesis 13:14,15).

We may ask: "To whom does the Land belong which God promised to Abraham? Are Abraham's descendants worthy of retaining it?"

Elijah once appeared to a poor but worthy man and said: "I am entrusting to your care a deposit which, if properly handled will make you rich, but after six years you must return it to me."

When Elijah returned to reclaim the deposit, the man revealed what he had done with the wealth he had accumulated, and showed Elijah receipts from hundreds of individuals and charitable institutions he had helped. Elijah was highly pleased and said: "You have so well administered the trust that you deserve to keep the original deposit."

So it is with the Jews in Israel. Many times has the question been debated: "To whom does Israel belong?" The Arabs maintain that the Land belongs to them because for many centuries they occupied it. But the *halutzim* (pioneers) declare: "See what we have done with the Land! For two thousand years the soil was neglected and became barren. We alone have made the country once more to flourish so that two million people can now live on it. We alone have given it the loving care it required. We have been true to our trust."

As one modern writer has expressed it: "Pagans, Christians, Mohammedans, Romans, Egyptians, Turks, Arabs—all in turn conquered the Land and tried to make it their own. But none succeeded. The Land waited patiently for her beloved sons. In the words of Israel Zangwill: 'The Land without a people waited for the people without a Land.' "

WHENCE AND WHITHER

The angel said: "Hagar, maid of Sarai, where have you come from and where are you going?" (Genesis 16:8).

Moses Mendelssohn, while out walking, was halted by a police officer who asked him where he was going, but Mendelssohn did not reply. The officer again asked him where he was going and, when he remained silent, arrested and jailed him. Hearing about this incident, the Kaiser hastened to the prison to release his friend.

"Why didn't you tell the officer where you were going?" he asked.

"I thought I was going to the Synagogue but you see I am here," replied Mendelssohn. "I have landed in prison."

"But why didn't you answer the officer when he asked where you were going?" the Kaiser persisted.

"Before I left home," Mendelssohn explained, "I read the week's portion of the Bible and came across this passage: 'An angel of the Lord found Hagar near a fountain of water in the wilderness and the angel asked: "Hagar, maid of Sarai, where have you come from and where are you going?" Hagar replied: "I am fleeing from my mistress Sarai."'

"The Bible tells us," continued Mendelssohn, "that Hagar answered only the first question: 'Where have you come from?' but not the second, 'Where are you going?' The truth is that no one knows where he is going. Hagar could not tell the angel where she was going nor could I tell the officer. We know whence we come but we do not know whither we are going."

Not knowing what lies ahead of us—the uncertainty of tomorrow—makes life interesting and challenging. Our destiny is in God's hands. We should so live today as to be ready to go wherever His will directs us on the morrow.

THE KADDISH LINKS THE GENERATIONS

I will maintain My covenant between Me and you and your offspring to come, as an everlasting covenant throughout their generations, to be God to you and your offspring (Genesis 17:7).

In twentieth century Europe, Ezra was for several years in a concentration camp. Finally liberated, he came to Israel to live in a youth village and there his teacher observed that Ezra seemed disturbed and was always sad. When the teacher gained Ezra's confidence, he learned that every night Ezra dreamed about his father who had died in a concentraiton camp. In this dream he saw his father always standing last in a long line of people, and always falling down. Then he heard his father's voice calling: "Why don't you help me? Can't you see I am falling? My son, why are you so far away?" Seeking Ezra's support, he held out his hand.

The teacher, wishing to help Ezra, sent him to the Curator of Mount Zion. After hearing his story, the Curator said: "Let's go to the Synagogue and pray. We are just in time for the evening service."

"But I've never prayed before," said Ezra.

"I'll help you," said the Curator. At the conclusion of the prayer, Ezra joined with the mourners in saying the *Kaddish*.

"Come and see me tomorrow," said the Curator. The next day, Ezra came into his office.

"What a difference!" Ezra exclaimed. "Last night I had a wonderful dream. My father again appeared but he was neither falling nor reproachful. Instead he was smiling and relaxed. I can't understand it. Was it perhaps because I said the *Kaddish* prayer?"

"There is nothing in the *Kaddish* about death," the Curator explained. "It is solely a prayer in praise of God. When a child recites *Kaddish*, he comes to realize that one generation is linked to another and that the responsibility of every generation is to praise God and help bring about His kingdom on earth.

"The mystics believe that when a man dies he is the last one standing in line to meet his Maker. Being the last one, he can easily fall backwards because there is no one behind him. Those who preceded him have the support of the one ahead and the one behind. When a son says *Kaddish,* he becomes his father's support and keeps him from falling.

"No superstition should be associated with the *Kaddish.* In the *Kaddish,* we exalt the Almighty and pray that God's kingdom may be established on earth in our lifetime and bring peace to all mankind. It is the *Kaddish* that reaffirms the covenant, and is the link which binds one generation to another."

TRUE HOSPITALITY

The Lord appeared to Abraham at the terebinths of Mamre as he sat at the entrance of the tent in the heat of the day. Looking up, he saw three men standing near him; and when he saw them, he ran from the entrance of the tent to greet them (Genesis 18:1,2).

If we carefully read these verses, it would appear that while Abraham was in the midst of talking to God, he left Him abruptly to welcome three strangers. The Midrash tells us that Abraham was not discourteous to God; he merely asked God to excuse him a moment so that he might extend hospitality to the wayfarers. The sages call our attention to the verse in the Talmud: *Gedolah kabalat orhim yoter mikabalat p'nay ha'shekhinah* "It is more important to accord hospitality to a human guest than to welcome God's Presence."

The story is told that the great Rabbi, Hofetz Hayim,* often invited strangers to his home for the Sabbath meal. On one occasion he learned that one of his guests had not eaten all day. The Hofetz Hayim omitted the *Shalom Alekhem* hymn which he usually sang at the table to welcome the heavenly messengers of peace, quickly chanted the *Kiddush,* and asked his wife to serve the food at once.

When the meal was over, the Rabbi sang *Shalom Alekhem,* the hymn which usually precedes the Sabbath meal. Then he sang his Sabbath table songs and finally presented his *D'var Torah* "a brief discussion of the Torah." When the stranger left, his wife asked him why he had changed his customary pro-

---

* Hofetz Hayim means "He loves life." (See Psalm 34:13-15.)

cedure. The Hofetz Hayim, replying that he had only followed the example of Abraham, quoted the above passage from Genesis and the Talmudic comment: "It is more important to accord hospitality to a human guest than to welcome God's Presence."

"You see," added the Rabbi, "we must first satisfy the hunger of a guest. The heavenly messengers of God who do not require food can wait to be welcomed after the meal."

WHO LAUGHS LAST

*And Abraham named the son who was born to him, whom
Sarah bore to him, Isaac (Genesis 21:3).*

Children are usually born while their parents are still young.
Yet when Isaac was born, his father Abraham was a hundred
years old and his mother Sarah, ninety.

When God told Sarah she would give birth to a child, she
laughed.

"How can I, who am so old, still have a child?" (Genesis
18:13). And Abraham also laughed.

Our Midrash tells us that even the angels laughed, as did all
the people who heard about it.

The first Jewish child was thus born amidst laughter. One
might suppose that his parents would have forgotten all this
laughter, but Abraham called the child, Isaac, a name derived
from the Hebrew root, "to laugh."

Now what is the meaning of all this laughter? Tradition tells
us that when Isaac was born, the whole world trembled; all
rulers and tyrants were frightened because they heard it ru-
mored that a child had been born who was to promulgate the
faith in one God. It was also prophesied that Isaac's descendants
would receive the Torah and sire the Prophets who would teach
the whole world justice, truth and mercy.

The tyrants, great and small, who ruled by force alone, naturally wanted to destroy this child, but their advisors allayed all
apprehensions when they asserted: "Abraham's son is never to
be feared. A child from such aged parents is bound to be a weak-
ling and can never grow up to be any threat to us. It's nothing
but a jest! Why, even his name is ridiculous. It means 'laughter.'" And in their ignorance they, too, laughed. Yet through
his son Isaac, Abraham's descendants became the great spiritual
teachers of mankind.

About eighty years ago, when the young Jewish pioneers, the
halutzim, first came to Palestine and talked of building an inde-

pendent Jewish State, the Turkish rulers of Palestine might easily have closed the doors to them. But the Turks simply laughed. What could a handful of Jews do in a country so arid, its climate intolerable, the whole land infested with malaria? Because these newcomers appeared to be so few and weak, the Turks allowed them to enter.

Among the Jews it was, however, no laughing matter. Their initial enterprise formed the nucleus of the *Bilu** movement that enabled these early settlers to establish thriving colonies which later comprised the foundation of what was to become the State of Israel.

When on November 2, 1917, Lord Balfour issued the famous Declaration bearing his name, promising Palestine as a homeland to the Jews, people everywhere laughed. Even Lord Balfour may have thought nothing would come of it. But out of this nothing was born a something, a reality, a regenerated nation.

When the United Nations voted to partition Palestine, seven neighboring Arab nations invaded this strip of land, but the Jews proclaimed the establishment of an independent Jewish State. Ernest Bevin, the then Labor Prime Minister, laughed. "The Jews will ask the British to return," he sneered. "What chance have they against seven Arab countries which vow they will drive the Jews into the sea?"

Seventy years ago, when Theodor Herzl wrote *The Jewish State,* the people laughed. Today the world is well aware that his dream was no laughing matter. His vision has been thoroughly vindicated through the establishment of *Medinat Yisrael,* the State of Israel.

"He who laughs last—!"

"When the Lord brought back those that returned to Zion . . . then was our mouth filled with laughter" (Psalm 126:1,2).

---

* The word *Bilu* is formed from the Hebrew initials of a verse in Isaiah (2:5) *Bet Ya'akov lekhu venelkha* "House of Jacob, let us rise and go."

THE WELL OF LIVING WATERS

God said to Abraham: ". . . . It is through Isaac that offspring shall be continued for you. As for Ishmael, the son of the slave-woman, him too will I make into a nation for he is your off-spring" (Genesis 21:12,13).

What merit was found in Isaac that he and not Ishmael should continue Abraham's spiritual heritage?

The answer appears in Genesis 26:18. "Isaac dug anew the wells of water which had been dug in the days of Abraham his father, and which the Philistines had stopped up after the death of Abraham." There is no mention anywhere that Ishmael dug anew his father's wells.

The well is a symbol of the Torah. In Numbers 21:17,18 we read: "Then Israel sang this song: 'Spring up, O well—sing to it —the well which the princes dug, which the nobles of the people delved with a sceptre and with staves.' "

Rashi explains that the princes are Moses and Aaron; the well is the Torah. Commenting on Isaiah 55:1, "Ho, everyone that thirsts, come for water," we are also told *en mayim ela Torah* "Water is interpreted to mean Torah."

Isaac reopened the same wells which Abraham had dug, and this implies that, like his father, he also studied Torah. Ishmael did not reopen the wells; he never studied Torah.

Each generation studies the Torah. The old wells are re-opened and in them we find fresh water with which to quench our spiritual thirst. We discover, as did our ancestors, new insights, new truths and fresh inspiration which makes the Torah "our well of living waters."

GOOD DEEDS BUILD GOD'S MOUNTAIN

God said: "Take your son, your favorite son, Isaac, whom you love, and go to the land of Moriah and offer him as a sacrifice on one of the mountains which I shall point out to you" (Genesis 22:2).

In commenting on the phrase, "the land of Moriah," the mystics tell us that the mountain which later was called Moriah was first a valley but later became a mountain. How do they explain this?

When Abraham and his son were on their way to "the land of Moriah" Isaac asked: "Father, where is the mountain? I don't see any mountain." Abraham replied: "My son, God will show us the mountain." The next day, Isaac spied a hill in the distance.

On the morning of the third day, the boy saw that the hill had become much larger and he was astonished.

"Why is it now so high?" he asked. "Is it because we are closer to it?"

"No, that's not the reason," said Abraham. "The soil on which we have been walking has miraculously been moved to Moriah and piled there, and all this has gradually built up the mountain. Every step we have taken has carried more soil to Moriah."

By the time they had reached it, Moriah had become a lofty mountain.

Great deeds are not accomplished in a moment, and true heroism is the accumulation of many lesser acts. Every step we take toward a great goal, every kindly deed we perform, every worthy sacrifice we make, help to form the mountain for the Temple of God.

EVERY DAY IS A DAY ON WHICH TO BE GRATEFUL

The span of Sarah's life was a hundred years and twenty years and seven years; these were the years of Sarah's life (Genesis 23:1).

Rashi interprets the phrase "These were the years of Sarah's life" as meaning *Kulan shavin l'tovah* "The years were equal in happiness."

But how can one assert that Sarah was really happy all those years? We know that Hagar and Ishmael caused her much pain and heartache. Moreover, our sages tell us that she died when she heard Abraham had taken Isaac to be offered as a sacrifice on Mount Moriah.

Rashi's interpretation was meant to point out that every one experiences sorrows as well as joys, and that we must accept everything Providence decrees for us. *Hayov adam l'vorekh al haraah k'shem shemevarekh al hatovah* "One is duty bound to praise God for the bad days as well as for the good" (*Berakhot* 33b).

A pupil once asked his teacher: "How can we praise God for the bad days in our lives?"

"You raise a difficult question," the teacher replied. "Go to Anapole and see Reb Zusa, a man who has suffered much; he will tell you." So the pupil went to Anapole and asked for Reb Zusa, but no one seemed to know him nor to be able to give any information about him.

Finally, an old woman told him that on the outskirts of the city lives a peddler by the name of Zusa. "Perhaps he is the man you are looking for."

The pupil went to Anapole and found Reb Zusa living with his wife in one room. Their clothing was shabby, the furniture

31

broken, and the only food on the table was stale bread and milk. Nevertheless, Reb Zusa welcomed him with the invitation: "Please sit down and have supper with us."

"No, thank you," said the visitor. "My teacher sent me here because he said you could explain to me the meaning of the Rabbi's teaching, that we must thank God for our bad days as well as for the good."

Reb Zusa seemed surprised. "I can't understand why your teacher sent you to *me*. I have never had a bad day in all my life. I am grateful for every day I live, no matter what it brings. To me every day is a day on which to give thanks and praise to God."

THE PRIVILEGE OF PERFORMING A MITZVAH

. . . *Rebekah went to the spring and filled her pitcher (Genesis 24:16).*

How did Eliezer know that Rebekah was the woman destined to be Isaac's wife? We are acquainted with the explanation given in the Bible (Genesis 24:12-15). But the Midrash quoted by Rashi, (Genesis 24:17) gives another reason: Eliezer saw that when Rebekah set down her pitcher to draw water, a strange phenomenon ensued—*She-alu hamayim likratah* "The water came up to meet her." That is why the Torah reads (Genesis 24:16): *vatmale* "the water filled her pitcher," not *vatishav* "she filled the pitcher." This was an indication that she was a *tzadeket* "a righteous woman."

When, however, Rebekah was asked by Eliezer for a drink of water, her offer to supply water to him and also to the camels is recorded not by the expression *vatmale* "the water filled up," but by *eshav* "I will draw the water." Why was it necessary for her to "draw the water" if the water came up to meet her?

Our sages explain that the water was about to rise up to her but Rebekah said: "If I am to perform a *mitzvah* and I can do it myself, I desire no help."

Rabbi Nahum of Chernoble had devoted his entire life to fulfilling the *mitzvah* of *pidyon sh'vuyim* "rescuing the captives and the imprisoned." His disciples offered to present him with a coach and horse so that he would not have to walk to perform this *mitzvah*. In refusing, he replied: "Why should I share the *mitzvah* with a horse? If a good deed is to be done, and I am able to do it myself, why seek assistance?"

THE MATERIAL AND THE SPIRITUAL

*. . . They called his name Esau. Then came his brother . . .
and his name was called Jacob (Genesis 25:25,26).*

Jacob and Esau represent two opposing concepts of life. This
is indicated in their Hebrew names. The Hebrew letters of the
name Esau may be read *osu* which means "they have made" or
"they have completed." This denotes that nothing more can be
done, and that one should be satisfied with what has already
been accomplished. The name Jacob comes from the root *akev*
which means "the heel of the foot"—at the bottom. It implies
that one is to grow, to develop and look upward.

Esau accepts the world as it is; all is well. But Jacob is not
satisfied with the world as it is. He recognizes that a great deal
remains to be done.

The difference between these two philosophies is also reflected in the blessing which their father, Isaac, conferred upon
them. Both were accorded the blessing of "the dew of heaven
and the fat of the earth." In the blessing to Jacob "the dew of
heaven" is mentioned first, and then "the fat of the earth"; but
Esau was blessed first with "the fat of the earth" and then "the
dew of heaven" (Genesis 27:28,39).

The order is most significant. If one is satisfied with the world
as it is and cares only for "the fat of the earth," material things
take precedence over all else; but if he strives for "the dew of
heaven," he will give priority to the spiritual values that exalt
life.

THE VIRTUE OF FORGIVENESS

Isaac loved Esau . . . (Genesis 25:28).

Isaac had two sons, Jacob and Esau. Esau was the unruly son, yet Isaac loved and forgave him. This has led our Rabbis to declare that Isaac, rather than Abraham or Jacob best understood and practiced the virtue of forgiveness.

The Talmud (*Shabbat 89 b*) bases this high estimate of Isaac on a fanciful interpretation of a difficult verse in Isaiah (63:16): "For Thou art our Father; though Abraham does not know us and Israel (Jacob) does not acknowledge us; but Thou, O Lord, art our Father, our Redeemer from of old is Thy name." How shall we interpret "Abraham does not know us and Jacob does not acknowledge us"? Why is Isaac's name omitted? Why is the phrase."Thou art our Father" repeated?

The Talmud explains that in the future God will reproach Abraham: "Your children have sinned against Me. What shall I do?" And Abraham will reply: "Let them be punished."

God will continue: "I will speak to Jacob who experienced the pain of rearing children; perhaps he will beseech mercy in their behalf." Thereupon God will say to Jacob: "Your children have sinned against Me." Jacob too will answer: "Let them be punished." God will retort: *Lo b'sabi ta'ama v'lo b'dard'ki etzah* "Old men (referring to Abraham) lack reason, and young people (referring to Jacob) lack counsel."

God will then say to Isaac: "Your children have sinned against Me. What shall I do?"

Isaac will reply: "Sovereign of the universe, are they *my* children and not *Your* children? When they accepted the Torah and said 'We will do and we will hearken,' You called them 'Israel, My son, My first-born' (Exodus 4:22; 24:7). Now You tell me they are *my* sons and not *Your* sons! Moreover, how much have they sinned? How many years does a man live? Seventy. You punished all who accepted the evil report of the ten spies except those under the age of twenty (Numbers 14:29). Subtract therefore twenty years during which man is not subject to punishment, and there remain fifty years; deduct twenty-five which comprise the nights when one sleeps and does not sin, and twenty-five years remain. Subtract twelve and a half years when a person works, eats, prays, etc., and twelve and a half years of life remain when one may sin. If You will forgive all their sins, well and good; if not, I will bear one half and You, the other. Should you say I must bear all, remember that I was willing to offer myself to You as a sacrifice."

On hearing Isaac's plea the people interpreted Isaiah's verse as follows: "You are our Father; Abraham does not know us, Jacob does not acknowledge us, but you, Isaac, are our father; you understand us, you ask that we be forgiven."

That is why the verse in Isaiah repeats: "Thou art our Father," once to refer to God, and the other to Isaac.

The Talmud continues that Isaac will say to the people: *Ad she'atem m'kalsin li, kalsu l'Hakadosh barukh ñu* "Instead of praising me, praise the Holy One, blessed be He."

This demonstrates that Isaac not only understood the virtue of forgiveness, but was also a man of great humility. The people who heard him, raised their eyes heavenward and exclaimed: "Thou, O Lord, art our Father, our Redeemer from of old is Thy name."

THE LADDER REACHING
FROM EARTH TO HEAVEN

Jacob dreamed and behold a ladder set up on the earth, and its top reached to heaven; and the angels of God were ascending and descending on it. And behold, the Lord stood beside him (Genesis 28:12,13).

Hebrew commentators frequently stress the symbolic significance of numbers. Before the Arabic system of numbers was in vogue, the Hebrews used the alphabet: *aleph* for one, *bet* for two, *gimel* for three, etc. The Hebrew word for ladder, *sulam*, spelled with a *vav*, has the numerical value of 136.

In the High Holiday prayers we read: "Repentance, Prayer and Deeds of Kindness annul the severity of judgment." In the old editions, the Hebrew word *tzom* "fasting" appears in small letters directly above the word *Teshuvah* "Repentance"; the word *kol* "voice" appears above the word *Tefillah* "Prayer"; and the word *mammon* "money" appears above the word *Tzedakah* "Deeds of Kindness." Each of the three Hebrew words, *tzom*, *kol* and *mammon* has the numerical value of 136, the same as in *sulam* "ladder."

צוֹם   קוֹל   מָמוֹן

וּתְשׁוּבָה וּתְפִלָּה וּצְדָקָה

מַעֲבִירִין אֶת רְעַ הַגְּזֵרָה.

According to commentators, this is to indicate that the ladder reaching from earth to heaven must be ascended through Repentance, Prayer and Deeds of Kindness. All three are essential; none may be neglected if we are to realize the hope of a better world for mankind.

THE SEARCH FOR ETERNAL LIFE

Jacob called the name of that place Beth El, but the name
of the city was formerly Luz (Genesis 28:19).

The ancients believed a legend that in Luz nobody ever died,
and many searched in vain for that place. The story is told about
Aaron, who heard that in Jerusalem there lived a wise man
called Naftali, who knew the location of Luz. Determined to
find Luz, Aaron went to Jerusalem, sought out Naftali and
asked him: "How can I get to Luz?"

Naftali did not reply at once but finally said: "Before you
can come to Luz you must find a town in the exact center of
which stands an old tree. There you will see Hayim, an old man
who will tell you how to reach the next town which also has a
tree standing in its exact center. There, another old man will
tell you how to get to the next town with a tree in its center.
In that town, an old sage with a snow-white beard will show
you a cave which must be traversed before you can find Luz.
There is no light in the cave but there are many passages. Only
when you have discovered the right passage will you find the
way to Luz."

Aaron at once set out to find a town with a tree exactly in its
center. He continued to follow Naftali's instructions until, after
several weeks had elapsed, he entered the cave. He took an
abundant supply of food with him because he had been warned
that the cave was vast, deep and long.

After wandering there for several days, he encountered an
old man.

"Shalom," said Aaron. "Who are you, my good man?"

"Menahem, son of Judah. And who are you?" the man asked.

They could not see each other because it was very dark in
the cave, but Aaron told him: "I am looking for the entrance
to Luz."

"The entrance? Strange. I am looking for the door to get out. Where is the door?" the man asked. "I must get out of here. I am so tired of Luz; I am bored to tears. There is absolutely nothing to do there."

When Aaron heard this he retraced his steps, left the cave, and returned to his home and the work that awaited him there.

Many imagine they would be happy if they could live forever. But without a purpose, without a sense of values, without a feeling of being wanted and needed, a protracted life would be boring, tedious and monotonous. Happiness is a by-product of the creative way of life. The zest and joy of life consists in service to others, in a feeling of usefulness and accomplishment, rather than the number of years one has lived or may live.

As someone has rightly said: "Adding life to our years is no less important than adding years to our life."

THE BLESSING OF TOIL

. . . Jacob served Laban another seven years (Genesis 29:30).

In Midrashic literature, Jacob is referred to as *bekhir she'b'-avot* "the elect of the patriarchs." Why did Jacob merit this recognition? Although he toiled seven years for Leah and another seven years for Rachel, we are told he was happy in all his labors. In ancient days, a man purchased his wife. Nowadays we say "a man takes a wife," but Jacob actually toiled for his wife. When we have to work to attain any objective, it becomes genuinely precious to us.

"When you eat of the labor of your hands, you are happy and it is well with you" (Psalm 128:2).

The only wall of the ancient Temple at Jerusalem which is still standing is the western wall known as The Wailing Wall. Why is this the only wall that remains? Based on the Midrash that God's Presence will never depart from the western wall, we are told in a legend that when the people were asked to construct the walls of the Temple, the wealthy chose the eastern wall and they hired workers to build it; the nobles preferred the southern wall and sent their servants to construct it; the rulers selected the northern wall and ordered their underlings to erect it. But all the others—the masses—built the western wall with their own hands. The eastern, southern and northern walls were destroyed, but the western wall, the product of people's actual labor and devotion, still remains.

Only that to which we give our own labor and devotion will endure and bring satisfaction and fulfillment.

FAMILY OR FRIENDS

*Jacob said to his brethren: "Gather stones." So they took
stones and made them into a heap; and they partook of a meal
there by the heap (Genesis 31:46).*

It should be observed that in this verse we are told that the
"brethren" worked and then feasted. Later in Genesis 31:54,
we note that the "brethren" did not work but feasted: "Jacob
then offered up the sacrifice on the mountain, and invited his
brethren to partake of the meal. After the meal, they spent the
night on the mountain."

Rashi points out that the "brethren" in verse 46 were Jacob's
sons—his own family who came to aid him in time of distress;
the "brethren" in verse 54 who feasted with him were merely
his friends.

When we invite people to a feast, everyone becomes our
friend, but when there is work to do, it is usually best to rely
on our own family.

FEARS THAT MAKE US HUMAN

Jacob was greatly afraid and distressed . . . (Genesis 32:8).

In the novel *Father and the Angels* by William Manners, we are told that when the mother learned that her son became a boxer she exclaimed: "He will be hurt." The father's reaction was: "He will hurt others." The father's attitude is in keeping with Jewish tradition.

When Jacob was about to meet Esau who was coming toward him with 400 men, the Bible tells us that Jacob was greatly afraid and distressed. Why does the Bible use two words "afraid and distressed" to express Jacob's emotion? Rashi explains that Jacob was "afraid" because he might be killed, and was "distressed" for fear that he might be provoked to kill Esau. The fear of being hurt is instinctive. We cultivate compassion and thereby become more humanized when we fear hurting others.

When God rebuked Cain for slaying his brother Abel, He said: "What have you done? Your brother's blood cries unto Me from the ground" (Genesis 4:10). The Hebrew word for "blood" is in the plural form. Rashi explains that by slaying Abel, Cain also slew Abel's unborn offspring.

This concept is prominent in Hasidism and in Jewish folklore. In *The Dybbuk,* for example, a man accused of cutting off the life of another in his prime is also held culpable for denying life to that man's unborn descendants.

The Talmud declares: "He who destroys a single human life is reckoned as if he has destroyed a whole world. He who saves a single human life is reckoned as if he has saved the whole world."

IDEALS DEMAND SACRIFICE

When Rachel was suffering in labor, the midwife said to her:
"Fear not for this is another son for you" (Genesis 35:17).

The mystics believed that Rachel's two sons were to be instrumental in bringing about the redemption of mankind. There was a tradition about a *Meshiah ben Yosef*, to the effect that "a Messiah would descend from Joseph," and that the Temple was to be built in Benjamin's domain. Moreover, the view was held that God entrusts every mother with the souls of the children she is to bear.

Rachel, it was said, had been entrusted with only one soul and that was Joseph's, but none was entrusted to her for Benjamin. She was, however, so eager to give birth to the second son in whose domain the Temple was to be built, that she gave her own soul to him so that Benjamin might be born. This is the meaning of the verse, "Rachel said to Jacob: 'Give me sons, or else I die' " (Genesis 30:1). She called her second son *Ben-oni* "son of my suffering," to indicate the sacrifice she had made that her son might live.

Rachel was the prototype of all those who give their own lives so that others may live.

CONSOLATION IN SORROW

And it came to pass, as Rachel was breathing her last—for she was dying—that she called his name Ben-oni, but his father called him Benjamin (Genesis 35:18).

It seems strange that Jacob, who so dearly loved Rachel, should have denied her dying wish to call their child Ben-oni. However, a wise psychological motivation prompted Jacob's action. If Rachel's child had carried the name Ben-oni "son of sorrow," he would always have remembered his mother's suffering. According to tradition, Jacob foresaw that the Temple was to be associated with Benjamin's name and would be built in his domain (Deuteronomy 33:12). Since the Temple must be associated with joy and not with sorrow, Jacob felt that his son should not bear a name reminiscent of suffering.

Another reason is advanced to explain why Jacob preferred not to name the boy Ben-oni. Rachel, realizing that her child would be orphaned and bereft of a mother's care and affection, bemoaned the fate that would destine him to sorrow. But Jacob sought to reassure his beloved Rachel that their son would never be neglected.

"I will call him Benjamin," he said, "which means 'The son of my right hand.' I will watch over him and always be at his side to help, comfort and guide him."

PERFECTING ONE'S CHARACTER

Jacob loved Joseph more than all his children because he was the son of his old age . . . (Genesis 37:3).

A man once asked his Rabbi how he might perfect his character. The Rabbi pondered for a while, then replied: "In the Bible, Joseph is called *ben zekunim* 'the son of his old age.' The *Baal Haturim* (Jacob ben Asher, the great fourteenth century Talmudic scholar and codifier) interpreted *ben zekunim* as an allusion to Jacob's transmission of the Oral Law to Joseph.

To understand what the *Baal Haturim* meant to imply, we need to know that the Oral Law which consists of the Mishnah and its commentaries, is divided into six "orders" or "sections."

Zayin, the first letter in the word *zekunim* is for the first section, *Zeraim* "Seeds" which deals with all agricultural laws and includes benedictions and prayers.

Kof, the second letter is for the second section, *Kodashim* "Hallowed Things" which deals with the offerings in the Temple service.

Nun, the third letter is for the third section *Nashim* "Women" which deals with betrothals, marriages and family relationships.

Yod, the fourth letter is for the fourth section *Yeshuot* "Salvation" which, according to the Talmud (*Shabbat 31 a*) is another name for the fourth section *Nezikin* "Damages" which deals with civil law and court procedure and includes *Pirke Avot* "Ethics of the Fathers." (*Nezikin* is referred to in the Talmud as *Yeshuot* "Salvation" because knowledge of this section saves men from encroaching upon their neighbor's rights or from allowing their own rights to be wrested from them.)

Mem, the last letter in the word *zekunim* is for the fifth section, *Moed* "Set Feasts" and comprises a discussion of all the holidays.

According to the *Baal Haturim's* interpretation, Jacob taught Joseph only five of the six sections. There is a sixth section in the Mishnah, *Tohorot* "Laws of Purity." Why was this section omitted from *Baal Haturim's* exegesis? This is to make clear that the knowledge of the Torah can be taught, but perfection of character cannot be imparted by study itself. There is a limitation to all teaching. The application of knowledge for improving one's character is a matter of self-training and self-discipline.

Joseph, the son of Jacob's old age, *ben zekunim* perfected his character through self-discipline. He soon outgrew the vanity displayed in his youth. In Potiphar's home, he resisted temptation, and in time of famine saved Egypt; he forgave his brothers and showed profound reverence for his father; and he exhibited true humility by attributing all his success to God. Joseph who acquired perfection of character is thus known as *Yosef Ha-tzadik* "Joseph the Righteous One."

AVOID PARTIALITY

Jacob loved Joseph more than all his children because he was a child of his old age; and he made him a coat of many colors (Genesis 37:3).

When making his last will and testament, a certain man wanted to leave most of his wealth to his favorite son. On hearing of this, his Rabbi strongly advised against such partiality because it would stir up strife among his other children and destroy their domestic tranquility.

"I see your point," said the man, "but can't I give him a special gift, some precious gem to indicate my great love of him?"

Warning him against even this partiality, the Rabbi quoted the passage from the Talmud: "A man should never single out one child among the others. Because Jacob gave Joseph two sela's weight more of silk than he did to his other sons, they became envious of their brother and the resulting chain of events brought about Jacob's descent into Egypt where his descendants remained for centuries in bondage" (*Shabbat 10 b*).

"Furthermore," the Rabbi continued, "you will be depriving your son of the love of his brothers who will probably no longer wish to acknowledge him as a brother. You will remember that, when Joseph's brothers brought his blood-stained coat to their grief-stricken father, they did not ask Jacob: 'Do you recognize *our brother's* coat?' but they asked: 'Do you recognize *your son's* coat?' (Genesis 37:32). They were so envious of Joseph that they hated him and no longer regarded him their brother."

THE EVIL OF SLAVERY

Reuben said: "Let us not take Joseph's life. Shed no blood. Cast him into this pit here in the wilderness" (Genesis 37:21, 22).

When Joseph's brothers conspired to slay him because they hated him on account of his dreams which they took to mean that he would rule over them, Reuben proposed that they cast Joseph into a pit. After this was done, Judah urged a different plan: "What profit is there," he said, "if we slay our brother and conceal his blood? Come, let us sell him to the Ishmaelites, and let not our hand be upon him for he is our brother, our own flesh." And his brothers listened to him (Genesis 37:26,27).

Since Judah was responsible for his brother having been sold into slavery, one would think that our sages might have said that we should be grateful to Judah because Joseph later became the Egyptian viceroy and saved from severe famine both the Egyptians and the Jews. The Talmud, however, approved of Reuben's action (*Makkot 10a*) not only because Reuben really intended to rescue Joseph and bring him back to his father (Genesis 37:22), but they wanted to make it absolutely clear that slavery is an evil which must at all times be condemned.

NOT BY MIGHT BUT BY MY SPIRIT

The seven lean cows devoured the seven fat cows (Genesis 41:4).

According to Hasidic lore, on one occasion the Jews complained to the angels: "God promised that we shall be an eternal people, yet He has given powerful weapons to many nations and none to us. How shall we be able to survive?"

On hearing this complaint, one of the angels answered: "When God created the animals He gave each a particular weapon. The lion He gave powerful paws; the tiger, sharp claws; the eagle, soaring wings; the serpent, fangs ejecting poison. But the little sheep who were not given anything, asked: 'What are You going to give us?' "

"Your weakness is your strength," replied the angel.

"How can that be?" asked the sheep.

"See that cedar," explained the angel. "How tall and strong it is! Now look at the reed by the lake. How small and feeble it is! But in a severe storm, what happens? The cedar is uprooted and the reed, having bent to the wind, remains unharmed. It is not always size and strength that assures survival."

Then the Jews understood. Babylon, Persia, Egypt, Rome, all in their day mighty powers, declined, became decadent and were destroyed. The defenseless Jews, without homeland or military forces have survived.

The *Sidrah Miketz,* recording the dreams of the seven lean cows that devour the seven fat ones, is always read during the week of Hanukkah. This is most apropos because Hanukkah tells the story of the Maccabees, when the strong were overcome by the weak and the many by the few. As history reveals, the weakness of the Jews became their strength and they compensated for this by developing greater resistance, endurance and spiritual depth.

"Not by might nor by power, but by My spirit, says the Lord of hosts" (Zechariah 4:6).

THE FEW SHALL PREVAIL

The seven lean cows devoured the seven fat cows . . . The seven thin ears of corn swallowed up the full ears (Genesis 41:4,7).

In ancient history as in our own time, in business, in politics, in war, and in many fields of human enterprise, the strong often prevail over the weak. Pharaoh's wise men, therefore, could not understand how the lean cows ever devour the fat cows—how the weak could triumph over the strong.

When the Torah portion dealing with Pharaoh's dreams is read on the Sabbath during the Festival of Hanukkah, we understand the power of the weak. When in 168 B.C.E. the mighty Antiochus attacked little Judea, many thought the outnumbered Jews would be quickly conquered. Their enemies had more powerful weapons and were far more experienced in warfare. But despite their weakness the Jews prevailed. We read about this heroic saga in the Hanukkah prayer *Al hanisim:* "Thou, O Lord, didst deliver the strong into the hands of the weak, the many into the hands of the few, the impure into the hands of the pure."

The Israeli War of Independence in our own day is a modern indication of this miracle. When the seven Arab nations invaded Israel, most observers thought it augured the end of the State of Israel. It was prophesied that the Arabs would drive the Jews into the sea. Nevertheless, the enemies were repulsed in accordance with the Biblical prophecy: "The Lord will cause the enemies that rise up against you to be routed before you; they shall come out against you one way and shall flee before you seven ways" (Deuteronomy 28:7).

When the few serve a righteous cause, they prevail over the many; when the weak are upright, they overcome the strong. The Prophet Zechariah (4:6) whose preachment is read on the Sabbath of Hanukkah, summarizes this truth in the memorable words: "Not by might nor by power, but by My spirit, says the Lord of hosts."

THAT NONE SHALL GO HUNGRY

It came to pass in the morning that Pharaoh's spirit was troubled (Genesis 41:8).

Pharaoh had two dreams. In the first, he saw that the lean cows devoured the fat cows. Then Pharaoh awoke. The Bible does not state that his spirit was troubled after this first dream. In the second dream he saw that the thin ears of corn swallowed the full ears. Then Pharaoh awoke. In the morning Pharaoh's spirit was troubled.

Since Pharaoh was not troubled by the first dream, why was he troubled by the second? As Joseph interpreted the first dream, it signified according to the Rabbis that the Egyptians would be deprived of all meat, a luxury that few could afford. They would, however, still have the necessities of life: fruits, vegetables, grain and bread. But when Pharaoh dreamed there would be no corn, he was greatly alarmed.

We can understand that a ruler naturally becomes apprehensive when his own subjects are in danger of starving for lack of bread. But it requires a far more sensitive and humanitarian spirit to be concerned over the starvation of people in other lands. Joseph possessed this humanitarian spirit. He feared that people outside of Egypt would also be without food; therefore, he opened his warehouses to help them.

The lack of food in underdeveloped countries throughout the world today must be the concern of all prosperous nations and they, like Joseph of old, should stand ever ready to help.

MELODIES BESTIR MEMORIES

Take of the choice fruit of the land in your baggage and carry it down as a gift for the man (Joseph) (Genesis 43:11).

What was it that so powerfully impelled Joseph to reveal his identity to his brothers? The Bible gives us to understand that it was the sight of his younger brother Benjamin, whom he so dearly loved and had not seen for many years. Joseph was also moved by the stirring plea of Judah who, having promised his father Jacob that he would bring Benjamin back, was now willing to serve as Joseph's slave instead of Benjamin. The Midrash points out that it was only when Joseph saw that his brothers were genuinely repentant that he decided to reveal his true identity.

We are told in Hasidic literature that when Joseph again heard the songs his shepherd father used to sing, they re-awakened memories of his childhood and inspired a yearning to become reconciled with his brothers. What were these songs? As a shepherd, when caring for his sheep, Jacob would sing one tune to gather them together; another when he led them to pasture; and still another when he brought them home. Joseph, his father's favorite, loved all these melodies.

When he saw his brothers the second time, what actually reminded him of these melodies? The Bible asserts that when Jacob finally consented to allow Benjamin to go to Egypt with his brothers to buy more grain, he said: "If it must be so, do this: take of the choice fruits of the land in your baggage and carry it down as a gift for the man."

But here the Bible employs an unusual expression for the "choice fruit of the land": *mizimrat ha-aretz* which literally means "from the songs of the land." Jacob had been singing Joseph's favorite songs and, according to the legend, the fruit had absorbed these melodies. Hence, when Joseph took the fruit from his brothers, he heard again his father's shepherd songs and his whole being was flooded with nostalgic memories of home and childhood. These reminiscences, coupled with his deep yearning and compassion, impelled Joseph to make himself known to his brothers and to effect a reconciliation with them.

Old melodies often revive memories of childhood, of home, of Synagogue and religion. The chants of Rosh Hashanah, Kol Nidre, the Torah Blessings and the Kiddush frequently stir the Jew to his depths and arouse nostalgia for the past. In after years, the lullabies and songs our mothers sang still reverberate in memory. The new songs that have come out of modern Israel have tremendously influenced our young people the world over. It has truly been said, "A people that sings, lives."

THE GREATER LOVE OF CHILDREN

When Jacob sees that the lad (Benjamin) is not with us, he will die (Genesis 44:31).

When the hidden cup was found in Benjamin's sack, Judah made a stirring plea to Joseph. Because it appeared that Benjamin would have to remain in Egypt and would not be permitted to return to his father, Judah said: "When Jacob sees that the lad (Benjamin) is not with us, he will die."

Benjamin already had ten children (Genesis 46:21). Why did not Judah say that if Benjamin did not return, his own children would die? It is because a father's love for his children is invariably stronger than children's love for their father. There is an old familiar saying: "One father can sustain ten children, but ten children cannot sustain one father." Why is this?

According to the Kabalists, all our human emotions derive from the first man, Adam, the father of mankind. Although Adam himself had no human father, he did have children. He could transmit to future generations the love of a father for his children but, because he himself did not have a father, he could not transmit to future generations the love of children for their father. In the Bible, they point out, there is no commandment that we must love our children; it is natural and instinctive to love them. We have inherited from Adam this natural affection. Only abnormal people have to be instructed to love their children.

It is true, the Ten Commandments do not tell us to love our children, but they do enjoin us to honor and love our parents. Love of parents is not instinctive; it must be indoctrinated, encouraged and cultivated. When Judah therefore pleads with Joseph that if Benjamin does not return with his brothers, he does not say that Benjamin's *children* will die, but that Benjamin's *father* will die.

THE STILL SMALL VOICE

The report was heard in Pharaoh's house: "Joseph's brothers have come." Pharaoh and his courtiers were pleased (Genesis 45:16).

The Hebrew word for "report," *kol* "voice," is written without the letter *vav*. Our sages tell us that the omission of the letter *vav* is to signify that the report of the brothers' arrival was not given in a loud voice. Yet it was loud enough to be heard in the palace.

A voice need not necessarily be loud. When Hannah prayed for a child, only her lips moved. Her voice was not even heard. The Priest in the Temple thought she was intoxicated, but God heard her and understood the depth of her desire.

The story is told of a child who went to the Synagogue to pray. Since he could not read, he whispered only those letters of the alphabet which he knew. In heaven, his prayer was heard and accepted.

How did God reveal himself to Elijah? God said to Elijah: "Go forth and stand upon the mount before the Lord." And behold, the Lord passed by and a great strong wind rent the mountain and broke in pieces the rocks before the Lord; but the Lord was not in the wind; and after the wind, an earthquake; but the Lord was not in the earthquake; and after the earthquake, a fire; but the Lord was not in the fire; and after the fire, a still small voice (1 Kings 19:11,12).

And the Lord was in the still small voice.

BE GRATEFUL AND REJOICE

The span of Jacob's life came to a hundred and forty-seven years (Genesis 47:28).

There is a legend that the three patriarchs, Abraham, Isaac, and Jacob should have lived the same number of years: namely, a hundred and eighty. Abraham, who died at a hundred and seventy-five, would have lived five years more had he not given five years of his life to a man who was very ill. Isaac lived the full hundred and eighty years. But Jacob lived only a hundred and forty-seven years—thirty-three years less.

For the explanation of this, we turn to the conversation between Pharaoh and Jacob. Pharaoh asked Jacob: "How many are the years of your life?" And Jacob replied: "The years of my wanderings are one hundred and thirty. Few and difficult have been the years of my life, and they do not equal the life-spans of my fathers in their wanderings" (Genesis 47:8,9).

The legend continues that after each of his words Jacob sighed. In heaven the angels were irritated that Jacob should sigh.

"Jacob, how can you say that your years were so few and difficult?" they asked. "You were saved from your brother Esau; God restored your son Joseph to you; all these years God has been with you and blessed you. Yet you complain that your life has been difficult. And how can you say you have not attained the years of your fathers? How do you know? You are still living; your life is not ended."

Because Jacob had sighed after each of the thirty-three words in his reply to Pharaoh, his span of life was reduced by precisely thirty-three years. And therefore he lived a hundred and forty-seven years.

From this it appears that Jacob was too concerned with the trials he had endured to remember all the blessings he had enjoyed. Instead of sighing over reverses and tribulations, one should be thankful and rejoice for the good he has had and the joys which may still come into his life.

56

WORTH RATHER THAN BIRTH

The younger brother (Ephraim) shall be greater than he (Manasseh) (Genesis 48:19).

When Joseph saw that his father was placing his right hand upon Ephraim's head to bless him, Joseph was displeased. He took hold of his father's hand to move it from Ephraim's head to Manasseh's, because Manasseh was the first-born. But Jacob, his father, objected: "I know, my son; I know. He too shall become a people, and he too shall be great. Yet his younger brother shall be greater than he" (Genesis 48:17-19).

Abraham had two sons, Ishmael and Isaac, but Isaac the younger, received the blessing. Isaac also had two sons, Esau and Jacob, but Jacob the younger was better qualified for leadership. Joseph had two sons, Manasseh and Ephraim, but Ephraim, the younger son, was destined to be greater. Moses was younger than Aaron, yet Moses was chosen to be the leader of the Israelites. Although David was the youngest of eight children, he was chosen to be King of Israel.

Our ancestors did not hold that because one is born first, he is therefore better qualified to do great things. Each man is to be judged solely on the basis of his own merit.

GOD DESIRES THE HEART

Moreover I have given to you rather than to your brothers, one
portion more which I wrested from the Amorites with my sword
and bow (Genesis 48:22).

Inasmuch as Jacob was not a soldier, how did he come to have
a sword and bow? The great commentator Rashi, interprets the
phrase "with my sword and bow" to mean "with wisdom and
prayer." Why is prayer symbolized by a bow? When we want
the arrow to fly far, we must pull harder on the string. When
the bow-string is held closer to the heart before it is released,
the arrow will soar higher and farther. So it is with prayer.
When it comes from the heart it soars upward to God.

There is a story told that on one Kol Nidre night when the
Synagogue was filled with worshipers and everyone was praying,
a shepherd boy entered. Although he knew no Hebrew, he
wanted God to hear his prayers, so with all his heart he blew
lustily on his reed. The congregation was shocked that anyone
should pipe a tune in the Synagogue, but the Rabbi declared
that because it came from the boy's heart, his piping was
precious to God.

Before a child can speak, he expresses himself through all
kinds of sounds, yet his mother understands him. Likewise,
when God's children speak to Him from the heart, however
imperfect their words, He understands them.

As the Talmud expresses it: *Rahmana liba bo-i* "God desires
the heart."

THE DEEPER MEANING OF THE ROCK

. . . The Rock of Israel (Genesis 49:24).

The Bible speaks of "The Rock of Israel." How and why was God designated as a rock or stone?

In the Bible, rocks or stones are frequently mentioned. When he dreamed of the ladder, Jacob had a stone for a pillow. He took many stones and placed them together for an altar. In ancient times, when a pact was made, the parties to the pact heaped up stones to signalize their agreement. The Ten Commandments were engraved on two tablets of stone. While the Israelites were fighting the Amalakites, Moses sat on a stone and prayed. The Psalmist speaks of "the stone which the builders rejected."

In the Hebrew word *aven* which means "stone" or "rock" there can be derived two words *av* "father" and *ven* or *ben* "son." When father and son are united in work or interests, their strength is like that of a rock. Happiness in family life is only to be found when parents and children are close to each other, when they do things together, when they are en rapport, and there is complete understanding between them. The secret of Jewish survival lies in the closeness of family relationship, in the ability of parents and children to walk together and cherish the same traditions and ideals.

Therefore, when the Bible refers to God as "The Rock of Israel" it denotes that God is the Father and His children are en rapport with Him: that He is their source of strength, and that they are to unite in carrying out His will.

שמות

Shortly after the Children of Israel left Egypt, where they had
been enslaved for centuries, they were confronted by fresh
dangers. Although the roaring sea on the horizon is terrifying,
Moses commands them to go forward. First to obey, the pioneer-
ing Nahshon ben Aminadav sets them an example of courage
and faith. The Children of Israel extend helping hands to each
other. This is the beginning of their feeling of unity and solidarity as a people. The crisis unites them.

And Moses stretched . . . . וַיֵּט מֹשֶׁה

out his hand over the . . . . אֶת יָדוֹ עַל-

sea and the Lord . . . . הַיָּם וַיּוֹלֶךְ

caused the sea . . . . . . ה״ אֶת הַיָּם

14:21   יד כ׳א

E X O D U S

THE CHALLENGE OF FREEDOM

*Now there arose a new king over Egypt who knew not Joseph
. . . Therefore they appointed taskmasters over the Israelites to
oppress them with forced labor (Exodus 1:8,11).*

This verse seems to imply that the Israelites were oppressed
because the new Pharaoh did not know Joseph. As a rule, Jews
were persecuted when they *were* known and became successful
in their business and professions. We might therefore suppose
that the persecution in Egypt would have begun because the
Egyptians *did* know Joseph and were envious of him.

But there is a deeper meaning in the verse, "The king knew
not Joseph." The truth is he did not know the character or
stamina of the Hebrews. When he oppressed the Israelites, he
was convinced they would become weaker; instead they became
stronger. "The more they afflicted them, the more they multiplied and spread out" (Exodus 1:12). It is a fact of human
nature that a virile people when oppressed may develop un-
suspected powers of resistance and new strength. This fact
Pharaoh ignored to his detriment.

Throughout their history, Jews have learned to overcome all
kinds of difficulties, to surmount obstacles and survive persecutions. Persecution is always a challenge. But for the Jews in
America and in other free countries, the challenge is to learn
how to survive in freedom, just as they have survived throughout centuries of persecution.

EXTENDING OUR HAND

. . . Pharaoh's daughter sent her handmaid to fetch the basket (Exodus 2:5).

When Moses lay in a frail basket amidst the bulrushes on the banks of the Nile, "the daughter of Pharaoh came down to bathe in the river and her maidens walked along by the river-side. She saw the basket among the reeds and sent her handmaid to fetch it."

The Hebrew word *amatah* which is usually translated "hand-maid" also means "hand." According to a legend, when Pharaoh's daughter saw the basket at a distance, she stretched out her hand to grasp it. Her handmaidens laughed and said: "You can't reach that basket; it's too far out." Pharaoh's daughter was at first embarrassed but in that moment a miracle occurred. Her hand began to stretch until it was long enough to reach the basket (*Talmud Sotah* 12b).

What seems too far away can often be reached if we will only make the effort to reach it. Distance is no obstacle where there is a will.

When the first *halutzim* "pioneers" came to Palestine people smiled, as did the handmaidens of Pharaoh's daughter. They asked: "How can these few ever build a Jewish homeland?" But the pioneers' vision of their redeemed ancient land was ever before them, athrob in their hearts, so that they extended their hands to redeem it. With the generous assistance of their fellow Jews all over the world, the pioneers translated their dream into the glorious reality—the State of Israel.

We are taught in our sacred literature *Kol hathalot kashot* "All beginnings are difficult." But once begun, they gather momentum that will hopefully lead to success. Appetites grow with eating; deeds grow with doing. "A journey of a thousand miles begins with a single step."

THE SILENT CRY

Pharaoh's daughter opened the basket and saw a child crying. She took pity on him and said: "This is one of the children of the Hebrews!" (Exodus 2:6).

Pharaoh's daughter did not *hear* Moses cry; she *saw* him crying. Our sages tell us that for three months, while Moses was hidden before being placed in the basket and set afloat on the Nile, the Egyptians had been searching for him as they did for all the new-born sons of the Israelites. From the outset, therefore, his parents had had to restrain him from crying to prevent his being discovered.

In Europe, during the Nazi holocaust, Jewish mothers were constrained to hide their children so that the Nazis could not find them. The young were taught not to cry aloud. They could shed tears, but they must not utter a sound.

One of the moving moments of Eichmann's trial concerned a witness who testified that, when the Nazis were defeated and the Jews liberated, a child asked her mother: "Mother, now may I cry out loud?" She did not ask: "Mother, may I now go out and play with my friends?" but "May I now cry out loud?" Could anything be more pathetic?

When we see a friend in dire need, although he may neither cry nor complain, we may be sure he is carrying his pain within him. If we know he needs help, why wait until he "cries out loud" before we provide help? Why wait until our people, or any needy people, cry out before we come to their aid?

WHO ARE YOU?

God spoke to Moses and said to him: "I am the Lord. I appeared to Abraham, Isaac and Jacob as El Shaddai, but by My name Adonai I did not make Myself known to them (Exodus 6:2,3).

Referring to the names, Abraham, Isaac, and Jacob, Rashi, the great commentator, says that these are the fathers—the patriarchs of our people. Is this not obvious? Rashi wanted to emphasize that Isaac was not only Abraham's son but was himself also a patriarch; Jacob was not only Isaac's son and Abraham's grandson but he too was a patriarch. Each was a father and a patriarch in his own right.

Sometimes when we ask a man his name, if his father is a prominent man, he may reply: "I am _____, the son of _____." But we are not really concerned with the father. We want to know "Who are *you?* What is your own *zekhut?* What is your own merit?"

There are those who speak proudly of a father or grandfather who was a learned man, who faithfully attended Synagogue services, who was generous and charitable. But what about themselves? Do they possess these virtues? Will their children be proud of them as they are of their ancestors? To these we can also say: "Who are *you?* What is your merit?"

IF THE PEOPLE DO NOT RESPOND

The Lord spoke to Moses, saying: "Go, speak to Pharaoh, King of Egypt, that he let the Children of Israel depart from his land." But Moses appealed to the Lord, saying: "The Children of Israel have not listened to me; how then shall Pharaoh hear me, a man with a speech impediment?" (Exodus 6:10-12).

Whenever he read this passage, Rabbi Samuel Moliver, an ardent Zionist, would sigh. "These verses puzzle me," he said. "Why did Moses argue with God? Why did he not try to find out what Pharaoh's reaction would be? Actually, I think these verses should be interpreted to mean that Moses said: 'What will happen if Pharaoh listens to me and agrees to let the Children of Israel go, but the Children of Israel refuse to hear me? I had better seal my lips and remain speechless.'

"This interpretation came to me," continued Rabbi Moliver, "when I considered recent events. After Theodor Herzl had finally persuaded the Turkish government to sell to the Jews a large tract of land in Palestine, he was thrilled by this diplomatic achievement. He appealed to Jewish philanthropists, and later to the Jews in general, for the necessary funds to make this purchase. He expected an immediate and overwhelmingly affirmative response. At long last, the Jews were to have the opportunity to return to their ancient homeland. But what did actually happen? The Turkish government listened and was willing to sell the land, but the Jews turned a deaf ear. Herzl, like Moses, was dismayed."

It is among the tragedies of history that often the most stubborn opposition to inspired leadership comes not from our enemies but from our own people. "They that would destroy and make you waste shall go forth from you" (Isaiah 49:17).

EVERY GENERATION MAY HAVE A MOSES

Amram took Jochebed, his father's sister, as his wife and she bore him Aaron and Moses . . . (Exodus 6:20).

In these simple words we are told of the birth of Moses, the greatest of the Prophets. In the same manner, we find reported in Exodus 1-3: "A man of the house of Levi married a Levite woman. The woman conceived and bore a son; and when she saw that he was a goodly child, she hid him for three months. When she could no longer hide him, she got a basket of bulrushes for him and daubed it with bitumen and pitch. She put the child into it and placed it among the reeds by the bank of the Nile."

Why is the story of the birth of Moses so simply reported? The birth of Greek and Roman heroes is almost always associated with supernatural events. In striking contrast, the Bible tells us of the humble origin of Moses in order to teach us that anyone, no matter how humbly born, may become a Moses or an Aaron. The birth of Moses is mentioned twice (Exodus 2:1-3; 6:20) to emphasize that Judaism does not attribute a supernatural origin to its heroes.

WE WILL GO WITH OUR YOUNG AND OUR OLD

. . . Pharaoh said: "Go, serve the Lord your God; but who are they that shall go?" And Moses replied: "We will go with our young and our old, with our sons and daughters . . ." (*Exodus 10:8,9*).

In Hebrew tradition, it was customary for the elders to precede the young so that, when the people heard Moses declare that the young were to go out of Egypt before their elders, they resented it. But Moses explained that the order of their going up to the Promised Land was to be the same as the order of their going down into Egypt.

The first to go down into Egypt had been the youth Joseph, who was followed by his father and older brothers. Liberation must also begin with the young. This was *midah k'neged midah* "measure for measure." For this reason, Moses had said: "Our young and our old will go up."

In our time, the return to Palestine has followed a similar pattern. First came the young people from Russia, Poland, and other lands. They developed the country and later their parents joined them.

Every Sabbath eve, parents who had recently arrived from Tunisia, Algeria, Morocco, and other lands offer a special prayer of thanksgiving to God because, fifteen years before, their sons had insisted on leaving for Israel. In all that time they had been unwilling to leave their homes and shops. But when conditions in these countries deteriorated, when their wealth was confiscated and conditions became unbearable, they finally emigrated to Israel where their sons are now able to help them establish new homes.

THE TORAH IS THE LIGHT

Moses stretched out his hand toward heaven, and for three days there was a pall of darkness throughout the entire land of Egypt. People could not see one another, and for three days no one could rise from his place; but all the Children of Israel enjoyed light in their dwellings (Exodus 10:22,23).

How do we explain that there was light for the Israelites and only darkness for the Egyptians? Based on a Midrash that compares Torah to light, the Hasidim tell us that the light came from within because the Israelites were constantly studying Torah.

The story is told that many years ago, when Palestine was under Turkish rule, a cruel Pasha forbade the Jews of Safed to kindle lights at night. Every evening the whole city, formerly illuminated by the light from the windows of houses in which diligent students were studying Torah, was completely shrouded in darkness.

But the windows of Rabbi Joseph Caro still glowed at night. It seemed as though he were defying the decree, and the defiance was spreading because night after night more and more windows were aglow, and the Torah chant was heard everywhere. When the lights grew brighter, the Pasha's guards reported to him these violations.

The Pasha, galloping at the head of his horsemen, furiously descended upon the Jewish quarter and stopped first at the house of Rabbi Caro, from which came the brightest light. Without knocking, he rushed into the Rabbi's house and beheld a strange sight. The Rabbi sat poring over his sacred Book; and the entire room was aglow with a luminescence that seemed to come from the walls although no lamp was burning.

The Pasha inspected the walls and saw they were covered with fireflies. When he demanded an explanation the saintly sage told him that during the day the room was thick with these insects, and in the twilight they shed light for him and also flew to every house in Safed where the Torah was studied.

"I don't understand," said the astonished Pasha. "Why do the fireflies spend the day in your room instead of absorbing the sunlight outdoors?"

With a twinkle in his eyes the Rabbi replied: "Evidently the Torah not only illumines the lives of those who study it, but also the fireflies who listen."

Observing the radiant affirmation in the saintly Rabbi's expression, the Pasha proclaimed a new decree.

"Light up your homes again! The old order is void. I can compel men to do my will, but this is beyond my power."

Wherever Jews study Torah, there is light.

THE HOPE FOR FREEDOM

In the first month from the fourteenth day of the month at evening, you shall eat unleavened bread until the twenty-first day of the month at evening (Exodus 12:18).

The observance of the Passover, the Festival of Freedom, begins on the evening of the fourteenth day of the month of *Nisan.* If for some valid reason it should be impossible to celebrate Passover on that date, the Bible says a *Pesah Sheni* "a Second Passover" may be observed one month later. This does not apply to Rosh Hashanah or Yom Kippur or any other holiday on the Jewish calendar.

Why is this exception made for the Passover? It is to teach us the vital importance of freedom which is never confined to any one time. It may be delayed for a while but it must come eventually; therefore we must never cease striving for liberty.

There is always a *Pesah Sheni.* In their long night of exile the Jews never relinquished their hope of returning to the land of their fathers. And because from generation to generation they clung to this hope, the dawn has broken and there has been created the State of Israel where at long last they shall live as free men in a democratic homeland.

Everywhere there is a deep yearning for freedom. Behind the Iron Curtain there are many who are oppressed and enslaved. For them, we hope there will be a *Pesah Sheni* "a Second Passover" when they shall be liberated and live in dignity as free men.

EXODUS 13:17—17:16

THE SONGS OF THE BIRDS

Then sang Moses and the Children of Israel . . . (Exodus 15:1-18).

The Sabbath on which we read the Song of Moses is known as *Shabbat Shirah* "The Sabbath of Song," and on this day it is customary to scatter crumbs to the birds. What connection is there between the birds and the Sabbath of Song? The great Hebrew poet, Bialik, wrote a charming poem entitled "To a Bird."

> Welcome! lonely bird, returning to my window . . .
> My soul has yearned for your sweet melody.
> Do you bring me greetings from my brothers in Zion
> Who are so far, yet so near? . . .

Thus does the poet welcome the birds who bring greetings from the Jewish Homeland.

There is a legend that, when David saw in a vision that the Temple was to be destroyed, he turned over to the birds his songs, the 150 Psalms he had composed. Because the Hebrew letters for 150 are *kof nun* and these two letters form the word *ken* which means "nest," David placed his songs in the nests and instructed the birds to fly out and sing his melodies far and wide.

And on the Sabbath of Song, we scatter crumbs to the birds so that they will come and sing us songs of Zion and bring us hope that redemption is near for all our brothers in every land.

THE EFFICACY OF PRAYER

It came to pass, when Moses raised his hand, that Israel pre-vailed (over Amalek); and when he lowered his hand, Amalek prevailed (Exodus 17:11).

Rashi asked: *Ve'khi yadov shel Moshe no'tzhot hayu hamil-hamah* "Was it then the hands of Moses that were winning the war?" And the exegetes explained: When Moses raised his hand in prayer, the Israelites were victorious, but when he lowered his hand and they ceased to pray, the Israelites suffered re-verses. Amalek is identified with Satan; when prayer is our ally, we can overcome even Satan.

An American woman was told by her physician that she would soon have to undergo a serious operation, but that this could wait until after her visit to Israel. Arriving in Jerusalem, she went to the tomb of David on Mount Zion and there offered a prayer for recovery. When she returned home, she went to the Synagogue and again prayed to the Almighty. After the opera-tion, her condition was critical, and for several days she hovered between life and death. She was asleep but her heart was awake in prayer.

In her delirium, this woman saw Satan enter her room and heard him complain: "Too bad! Too bad! I cannot do anything here! There are too many prayers. I cannot get through!" After the crisis, she began to feel better, regained her strength and was soon completely recovered.

Again she went to the Synagogue to offer prayer—but this time a prayer of thanksgiving.

THE PLEDGE AT SINAI

. . . All that the Lord has spoken we will do (Exodus 19:8).

The story is told that when Count Valentine Potocki of Wilna, after a thorough study of the Jewish religion, was converted to Judaism, the Wilna Jews feared this might be an excuse for a pogrom against them. A delegation of Jewish leaders therefore visited the Count and asked him to consider returning to his former religion.

He refused in these words: "According to Jewish tradition, not only the 600,000 Israelites stood at the foot of Mount Sinai to receive the Torah, but also all the unborn generations of mankind. God asked the Gentile nations to accept the Torah and they refused. But when He asked the Children of Israel they replied: 'All that the Lord has spoken we will do.' Thereupon God gave the Torah to the Children of Israel.

"Did *all* the unborn generations of Gentiles at Mount Sinai say 'No'? By no means. I was one of those who cried out 'Yes!' I accepted the Torah and I will have no peace unless I live by it."

If Count Potocki felt that he was among the unborn at Sinai who had agreed to accept the Torah, each Jew of our day must feel that he also was present at Mount Sinai and heard the memorable Ten Commandments. He, too, voiced with his ancestors the pledge: "All that the Lord has spoken we will do." That pledge must never be forgotten. We must constantly affirm and reaffirm it.

MOUNT SINAI, AN HISTORICAL THEOPHANY

Mount Sinai was all in smoke . . . (Exodus 19:18).

During the Israeli Sinai campaign, many thought they might be able to locate Mount Sinai where Moses had proclaimed the Ten Commandments. A delegation came to the Curator of Mount Zion and asked him to bless their efforts to find the holy Mount Sinai. He refused, claiming that, in the first place, Mount Sinai was no longer holy. Before the Ten Commandments were delivered there, the mountain had always been considered so holy that people were warned against even touching it. God said to Moses: "You shall set bounds for the people all around, saying: 'Beware of going up the mountain or touching the border of it. Whoever touches the mountain shall be put to death'" (Exodus 19:12). But after Moses had received God's revelation, Mount Sinai was no longer considered holy. *Hemah ya'alu bahar*—"Then they could ascend the mountain" (Exodus 19:13).

The Curator went on to explain that, in the second place, no one could ever find the physical Mount Sinai because it no longer exists. According to legend, all the mountains of the world coveted the honor of being the locale for the revelation of the Ten Commandments. To placate all of them, God took some soil and rock from each mountain and out of them formed Mount Sinai. The Ten Commandments were proclaimed on the part taken from Mount Moriah, where Abraham had brought Isaac to be sacrificed. However, after the revelation of the Torah to the Children of Israel, God returned to all the mountains the portions He had borrowed from them; therefore Mount Sinai no longer exists. Thus Sinai was an historical event rather than a geographical locale.

Some believe that, even as the soil of Mount Moriah was returned from the desert to the Holy Land, so whatever Torah scholarship and erudition Jews may produce in the Diaspora must eventually be transplanted to the Holy Land. The great *Yeshivot* (Academies) of Slabodka, Wilna, Lublin and others are no longer in Poland or Russia. They have been transferred to Israel. Indeed, "out of Zion shall go forth the Torah and the word of the Lord from Jerusalem."

THE RABBI'S COMPANION IN PARADISE

Honor thy father and thy mother . . . (*Exodus 20:12*).

A renowned Rabbi was extremely anxious to know who would be his companion in Paradise. One night he dreamed that the angels showed him Paradise. Taking him to a room containing a chair, a table, a crown and the sacred Books, one of the angels said: "This is your place."

"Now," said the Rabbi, "I would like to know who is to be my companion." Before the angel could reply, the Rabbi heard the neighing of a horse.

"What's that?" he asked as he saw a horse, drawing a coach, come galloping toward the room. In the driver's seat sat a man with a whip, shouting: "Whoa! Whoa!" How amazed was the scholar when the angel told him this coachman was destined to be his companion!

"But I don't understand," he said. "Who is this man and where does he live?"

"He is Nuless from Lublin," the angel replied. Then the Rabbi awoke from his dream.

On the following day, the Rabbi traveled to Lublin and asked everyone there: "Is there a man here by the name of Nuless? Where can I find him?" The people, surprised that such an eminent Rabbi should be inquiring about Nuless, nevertheless sent for him. But Nuless told the messenger that he could not come.

When a second messenger was sent, Nuless said to him: "Tell the Rabbi I can't come to see him. If the Rabbi wants to see me, please tell him I shall be at home all day." The people were incensed at his audacity and asked: "How can a man like Nuless refuse to come to the great Rabbi?"

Nevertheless, the Rabbi went to Nuless's home, and when Nuless saw him, he apologized and explained:

"My mother is very sick and I have no one to take care of her; therefore I must stay here with her all day. In the early evening when she is asleep, I take my horse and coach and try to pick up some fares to make enough to provide her with food. I've had to do this for the past ten years."

The Rabbi now understood why Nules was worthy to be his companion in Paradise.

That very day the Rabbi preached to his congregation on the theme: How great is the *mitzvah* of honoring one's parents. He who honors his father and mother will surely have a place in Paradise.

Respect for parents is the foundation of the family, and the family is the foundation of society. According to the Talmud, God says: "When a man honors his father and mother, I dwell in his house" (*Kedushin 36*). Wherever there is respect for parents, there is also respect for authority and the nation is strong.

ENTHUSIASM MUST BE CONTINUOUS

And these are the ordinances which you shall set before them (Exodus 21:1).

The conjunction "And" in this verse connects the Ten Commandments in the preceding *Sidrah Yitro* (Exodus 18:1-20:23) with the detailed laws that follow in the *Sidrah Mishpatim* (Exodus 21:1-24:18). It is noteworthy that the enthusiastic response of the Children of Israel, "We shall do and we shall obey" does not follow the Ten Commandments in the *Sidrah Yitro* but is found in this *Sidrah Mishpatim* (Exodus 24:7). The fact that this enthusiastic response came later seems to indicate that enthusiasm must not only be for the moment but must be continuous; therefore, the conjunction "and" is to signify this continuity.

A Bar Mitzvah is thrilled on the Sabbath when he is called to read from the Torah. This is a great moment in his life, and he is particularly happy because his relatives and friends have come to the Synagogue to witness this joyful occasion. But unless his enthusiasm continues, the Bar Mitzvah ceremony loses its meaning.

We read in Psalm 34:12: "Go, children, hearken unto Me; I will teach you reverence for God." The verse does not say *Bo-u* "Come" but *L'khu* "Go." The meaning is: "You shall hear Me not only when you are here but also wherever you go." Enthusiasm must be continuous.

KEEP FAR FROM FALSEHOOD

Keep far from falsehood . . . (Exodus 23:7).

Why does not the Torah simply state "Do not lie"? What is the significance of the word *tirhak* "Keep far (from falsehood) "?

In our folklore we are told that one of the functions of the Prophet Elijah is *l'rahek hamkurabim* "to separate some who are close," and *ulkarev hamruhakim* "to bring near those who are separated." What does this mean?

Ishmael had exercised a bad influence upon Isaac and it was Elijah who caused them to be separated. Likewise, Laban and Jacob, having nothing spiritually in common had to be separated. But when a father is estranged from a son, or a husband from a wife, Elijah's function is to bring them closer so that they may be reconciled.

The Hebrew word *sheker* meaning "a lie" or "falsehood" is spelled *shin kof resh*. These three letters follow each other in the Hebrew alphabet. The three letters of the word *emet* "truth" are widely separated. The *aleph* is at the beginning of the alphabet, the *tav* at the end, and the *mem* in the middle.

It is important to separate the letters in *sheker* because we are told "to keep far from falsehood." Conversely, we must bring together the *aleph mem* and *tav* in the word *emet* so that truth may be brought closer.

The mystics also say that when Elijah will come, he will re-arrange the letters of the alphabet, separating those which spell *sheker* and bringing close the letters in *emet*. The Talmud tells us: *Hotmo shel Hakadosh barukh Hu emet* "Truth is the seal of God." Thus will truth keep all mankind far from falsehood as our Torah commands.

There is another interpretation of the arrangement of the letters in the word *emet*. Some think that truth is at the extreme right, like the letter *aleph* in *emet*; others maintain that truth is at the extreme left, like the letter *tav*. Still others claim that truth is somewhere in the center, like the letter *mem*. The fact is that truth is not to be found at either extreme, but by bringing together the right, the left and the center.

INSPIRATION MUST BE RETAINED

The Lord said to Moses: "Come up to Me on the Mount, and wait there; I will give you the tablets of stone with the laws and commandments which I have inscribed, that you may teach them (Exodus 24:12).

Moses was on the mountain with God for forty days. It was not enough for Moses to ascend the mountain; he had to remain there. The Psalmist asks: "Who shall ascend the mountain of the Lord and who shall *stand* in His Holy Place?" (Psalm 24:3). It is not enough to climb the mountain. The verse specifically says: *umi yokum* "who shall *stand* there?" The inspiration we have gained must last. Man must retain the inspiration he receives.

It is one thing to make a dramatic ascent; it is another to remain on the heights. Moments of inspiration must not be lightly taken; they must be translated into the round of daily living.

Ma'alin bakodesh v'lo moridin "In our sacred experiences, we must climb higher and higher, and never slip back."

TAKE GOD INTO YOUR LIFE

The Lord spoke to Moses saying: "Speak to the Children of Israel that they take for Me an offering from every person whose heart so moves him" (Exodus 25:1,2).

We can find an interesting connection between this *Sidrah Terumah* (Exodus 25:1-27:19) and the two preceding *Sidrot, Yitro* (Exodus 18:1-20:23) and *Mishpatim* (Exodus 21:1-24:18).

In *Yitro* we learn that God gave the Torah to the Children of Israel. From this we may infer that God said: "The Torah is Mine; it is one of My most valuable possessions, but I give it to you. Take it."

The *Sidrah Mishpatim* concerns itself with justice. We are told: *Ki lekha Adonai hatzdakah* "For Justice is Thine, O Lord." But God said: "Justice is Mine, yet I give it to you. Take justice."

In *Terumah* we read: "Take for Me an offering." Since obviously God does not need offerings, we might substitute *v'yikhu oti* in place of *v'yikhu li*, and the phrase would read: "Take Me!"

According to this, we may deduce that God said to the Children of Israel: "You have the Torah and you have justice. Now take *Me* into your life."

If man holds fast to the knowledge and wisdom of the Torah; if he makes justice the basis of all his actions; if God and religion are vital to him, then his life is complete.

The Kotsker Rabbi was asked: "Where do you find God?" And he answered: *Avu men lost Ihm arein,* "Wherever He is admitted, there God is to be found."

SUPPLYING THE MATERIAL

They shall make an Ark of acacia-wood . . . (Exodus 25:10).

The Midrash asks: "Where did the Children of Israel obtain the wood for the construction of the Ark and the furnishings of the Tabernacle? They were in the desert on the way to the Holy Land, and there are no trees in a desert. Where then did they get wood?"

There is an old legend that when Jacob went down into Egypt, he planted trees. He was asked: "Why are you planting trees? Do you intend to remain in Egypt instead of returning to your native land?"

"I am planting trees," he replied, "so that, when the Children of Israel leave Egypt, they may cut the trees for wood and take the wood with them for the *Mishkan* 'the Tabernacle.'"

According to this legend, Jacob must have foreseen that the building of Jewish institutions in Israel would require material which could only be obtained from Jews in the diaspora. And thus, from Jewish communities throughout the world have come the resources with which to build not only Houses of Worship and *yeshivot* "schools of learning," but also hospitals, universities and all other necessary institutions.

ALL MUST BUILD THE ARK

They shall make an Ark of acacia-wood . . . (Exodus 25:10).

It is significant that the command *V'asita kaporet* "You shall make the cover for the Ark" (Exodus 25:17) is in the singular. The commands *v'asita shulhan* "and you shall construct the table" (Exodus 25:23), and *v'asita menorat zahav* "and you shall design the menorah of gold" (Exodus. 25:31) are also in the singular. This singular form *v'asita* occurs twenty-nine times in this *Sidrah* in connection with the construction of the various details of the Tabernacle. But the command *v'asu Aron* "and you shall build the Ark" (Exodus 25:10) is in the plural.

A single individual can make the various furnishings of the Tabernacle, but the Ark must be made by all the people. The Ark which houses the Torah involves the efforts and responsibility of the entire community. The teachings of the Torah are to be cherished both individually and collectively.

We do not know where the original Ark is, but the spiritual Ark must be within us. We are the Ark. By studying and following its precepts, we carry the Torah in our hearts. The Ark is perfected through the combined efforts of all.

THE TWO CHERUBIM

*You shall make the cherubim of gold . . . Make one cherub
at one end and one cherub at the other end of the Ark-cover
. . . And the cherubim shall spread out their wings upward
. . . They shall face one another . . . There will I meet with
you and speak with you from above the Ark-cover, from between the two cherubim which are upon the Ark . . . (Exodus
25:18-22).*

When the High Priest declared the word of God to the people, he stood near the cherubim because, according to Verse 22,
God's voice issued from between them. The wings of the cherubim were spread toward heaven and the cherubim faced one
another. The wings spreading toward heaven symbolized the
importance of *mitzvot ben adam lamakom* "duties of man to
God." Because the cherubim faced each other they symbolized
the importance of *mitzvot ben adam lahavero* "duties of man
to his fellow."

The childlike countenance of the cherubim were also symbolic. God speaks from the place on the Ark-cover where the
cherubim appear as children. The High Priest was to begin
with the children, to teach them to love God, to love man and
to observe the teachings of the Torah.

The Rabbi of today stands in the place of the High Priest of
old, and like the High Priest, his task is three-fold: to teach the
duties of man to God; to teach the duties of man to man; and
to instruct the children to walk in the ways of God.

SPACE EXPANDS AS FRIENDSHIP GROWS

*There I will meet with you and I will speak with you from
above the Ark-cover . . . (Exodus 25:22).*

We have been told by our wise men that two people who
love each other can live together even on the edge of a sword.
But when there is dissension, the entire world is too small.
When the Children of Israel were in the desert, a small Ark
sufficed for them as symbol of their religion. God could meet
with them there.

In striking contrast, due to occasional internal dissension,
God's spirit did not always dwell in the magnificent Temple
of Solomon. Isaiah declared (66:1): "Thus says the Lord: 'The
heaven is My throne and the earth is My footstool; where is the
house that you would build for Me? And where is the place
that may be My resting place?' "

The size of a Synagogue is not important, but rather the
spirit that permeates it. If the Synagogue promotes friendship,
understanding and holiness, God's spirit abides there.

While riding in his coach, a Hasidic Rabbi saw a friend, walking along the road. He told the coachman to stop, and invited
his friend to ride with him. "Thank you," said his friend, "but
there is room for only one in your coach; I do not want to in-
convenience you."

"Where there is friendship, there is always room," replied
the Rabbi.

In former generations many families lived in small quarters,
but in the humblest home there was always room for an *orah*
"a wayfarer." A stranger attending the evening service in the
Synagogue was invariably invited to join some family for his
meals and lodging. Nowadays, most of us live in large quarters
but we seldom if ever invite an *orah* to be our guest for the
night.

The State of Israel has been accused by the Arabs of coveting more territory at the expense of its neighbors. But Israel replies to this accusation:

"Although we have already absorbed two million, we have enough land for more. This small land which has been neglected for centuries can, through scientific irrigation and loving care, absorb an additional three million."

Even in a small country, where there are common national goals, mutual respect, friendship and camaraderie there is always ample room.

MOSES'S NAME OMITTED

The weekly Portion Tetzaveh (Exodus 27:20-30:10).

The name of Moses does not appear even once in the entire *Sidrah Tetzaveh*. Our Rabbis explain this omission as follows: When Moses saw that the Tabernacle was already built, he thought he should step aside because the people no longer needed him as a leader.

"You now have the Tabernacle," he said. "You don't need me." So his name was left out of the *Sidrah Tetzaveh*.

But Moses soon realized that this did not hold true because, in the absence of their leader, the people lost faith, fashioned and worshiped the golden calf. Had Moses been with them, and not on the mountain, they might never have committed this sin. The omission of the name of Moses is intended to emphasize that a leader is indispensable.

It is said that in the days of Esther and Mordecai, the people resented the omission of Moses's name from this *Sidrah* which, except during a Leap Year, is read before Purim.

They declared: "Moses made great sacrifices for his people and yet God omitted his name from the *Sidrah Tetzaveh*. When the Book of Esther is written, God's name will be omitted. This will indicate that we consider that a leader is to be recognized and appreciated."

FOR BEAUTY AND FOR DUTY

You shall make sacred garments for your brother Aaron, for dignity and beauty. You shall instruct all who are wise of mind, whom I have filled with the spirit of wisdom, that they may make Aaron's garments for consecrating him, to serve Me as Priest (Exodus 28:2,3).

The garments of the Priest have a two-fold purpose or function. They were to be beautiful and they were to impress upon the Priest his duty; therefore, there are two verses concerning these garments, one stressing their beauty and the other, their holiness.

Speaking of the ephod and the robe, our sages declare that they were not only to be beautiful, but also to have an ethical purpose: *neged lashon hara,* to remind us "to avoid evil gossip."

The *Tallit* "prayer shawl" is not only to be decorative, but its fringes, according to the Bible, are to remind us of God's commandments which we are to obey.

The *mezuzah* on our doorpost should not only be attractive but should serve as a constant reminder that the home is to be filled with God's spirit. "Except the Lord builds the house, they labor in vain who build it" (Psalm 127:1).

The *Sukkah* "booth" should not only be beautiful but recall the protection which God gave our people in the wilderness and cause us to offer thanksgiving for all the bounties with which God has blessed us.

The Sabbath candlesticks, *kiddush* cup, *hallah* cover, *havdalah* candle and the *besomin* box are not only intended to add charm to the Jewish home, but to bring it the joy and peace of the Sabbath.

The Hanukkah menorah is not only an art object but it is to be illuminated and call to mind the victory of the Maccabees in their struggle for religious freedom.

STONES WITHOUT LETTERS ARE HEAVY

The Lord spoke to Moses: "Go down, for your people whom you brought out of the land of Egypt have dealt corruptly. They have turned aside quickly from the way which I commanded them; they have made themselves a molten calf and have worshiped it, and have sacrificed to it, saying: 'This is your god, O Israel, who brought you out of the land of Egypt.' " And the Lord said to Moses: "I see that this is a stiffnecked people" (Exodus 32:7-10).

It seems strange that Moses did not shatter the tablets of the Law as soon as he heard that his people had made a molten calf and were worshiping it. It was only later in verse 19 that Moses cast them down and "shattered them at the foot of the mountain." Why didn't Moses break them immediately after God told him what had happened? Did he disbelieve what God said? Did he have to see with his own eyes that the Children of Israel were dancing around the golden calf?

The mystics tell us that because they contained the Word of God, Moses did *not* break the tablets, but when he descended from Sinai, the letters on the tablets saw the dancing and debauchery and became so irate that they flew back to heaven. Denuded of the letters, the stone tablets became too heavy for Moses to carry. They fell down and were shattered.

So it is with Judaism. Judaism can become burdensome only to those who are carrying tablets without letters, obligations without understanding. When Judaism becomes meaningful the tablets are no longer onerous. We are told that when the tablets contained the Word of God they were not too heavy for Moses to carry. *Haluhot nosim et Moshe* "The tablets carried Moses."

When we adhere with fidelity to God's Word, His Torah will carry us. When we are dedicated to an ideal, the ideal itself will sustain and uplift us. No task will be too difficult, because the spirit is winged.

THE LEADER NEEDS THE PEOPLE

The Lord spoke to Moses: "Go down, for your people whom you brought out of the land of Egypt have dealt corruptly. They have turned aside quickly from the way which I commanded them; they have made themselves a molten calf and have worshiped it, and have sacrificed to it, saying: 'This is your god, O Israel, who brought you out of the land of Egypt.'" And the Lord said to Moses: "I see that this is a stiffnecked people" (Exodus 32:7-10).

This passage voices a direct rebuke to Moses. The people whom he led were stiffnecked. But why should God have rebuked Moses? Since he was on Mount Sinai when the Israelites sinned, how could he be blamed for the sins of his people? We would think that, instead of being reprimanded, Moses should have been encouraged by God to have patience with such a people.

The answer is: *Shakul Moshe keneged shishim ribbo* "Moses was equivalent to the six-hundred thousand Israelites"; he was the personification of the people with all their virtues and failings. And Moses knew that, as their leader, their sin was his sin, because he bore the responsibility for any misdeed of those whom he led.

"If now I have found favor in Thy sight, O Lord, let the Lord, I pray Thee, walk in our midst; for it is a stiffnecked people; and pardon *our* iniquity and *our* sin, and take us for Thine own " (Exodus 34:9).

Moses did not commit the sin, yet he said: "Pardon *our* sin, pardon *our* iniquity." When the people reach great heights, so does Moses. When the people are wicked, Moses falls and is implicated in their sin. Leaders can only rise or fall as their people rise or fall.

People need leaders to guide, instruct and inspire them and, conversely, the leaders need the people. A great leader can only succeed when the people are faithful to his leadership.

STUBBORNNESS—VIRTUE OR VICE

The Lord said to Moses: "I see that this is a stiffnecked people" (*Exodus 32:9*).

Stubbornness may be a virtue or a vice. Stubborn hope, faith and courage are all commendable. But stubborn rage, doubt, prejudice and sinfulness are both dangerous and destructive.

The stubborn determination to refuse on the Sabbath any engagement that will prevent attendance at Synagogue services is certainly praiseworthy. But to stubbornly refuse to contribute to an institution because of some slight by an officer or member is petty and destructive.

The pioneers in Israel could never have succeeded if they had not been stubborn in their determination to develop the land. If he had not stubbornly refused to speak any other language than Hebrew in the Holy Land, Ben Yehuda could never have succeeded in making Hebrew a living tongue.

THE WORK OF OUR OWN HANDS

The Lord said to Moses: "Carve two tablets of stone like the first and I will inscribe upon the tablets the words that were on the first tablets which you shattered" (Exodus 34:1).

Why did God tell Moses who had broken the first tablets to prepare another pair? Had the people suddenly changed for the better? If they still worshiped the golden calf, why should Moses now make new tablets?

God Himself had made the first tablets and they were now broken; therefore He bade Moses: *P'sal lekha "You* carve two tablets." There is this explanation: what a man makes himself he is generally zealous to preserve. The Midrash, in commenting on this incident (also described in Deuteronomy 10:1), asserts that God said to Moses: "You broke the tablets because they were the work of *My* hands. Now make your own, and you will not break them."

A similar reason is given for the survival of the western wall of the Temple at Jerusalem. Why did this one wall remain? The eastern wall had much more significance because the Jews always prayed facing toward the east. If one wall was to remain, why was it the western wall?

Based on the Midrash that God's Presence will never depart from the western wall, we are told in a legend that when the people were asked to construct the walls of the Temple, the wealthy chose the eastern wall and they hired workers to build it; the nobles preferred the southern wall and sent their servants to construct it; the rulers selected the northern wall and ordered their underlings to erect it. But all the others—the masses— built the western wall with their own hands. The eastern, southern and northern walls were destroyed, but the western wall, the product of people's actual labor and devotion, still remains.

Only that to which we give our own labor and devotion will endure and bring satisfaction and fulfillment.

THE SABBATH AND THE SIX DAYS OF THE WEEK

Six days shall work be done, but the seventh day shall be a Sabbath of complete rest, holy to the Lord . . . (Exodus 35:2).

There is a close relationship between the six weekdays and the seventh day, the Sabbath. In six days God created the world by His Word. Since God rested on the Sabbath day, how was the Sabbath created? From Jewish folklore we learn that when the world was created, the Sabbath had as yet no life or existence. How then did the Sabbath come into being? In ancient days each of the six days had twenty-eight hours. When they saw that this seventh day needed hours in order to live, each day contributed four of its hours so that the Sabbath could have twenty-four hours of life.

Thus we are told that the Sabbath exists only through the contribution of the other six days. When love, kindness and honesty prevail on the six days of the week, then the Sabbath day is holy. But we cannot feel the peace of the Sabbath if, during the six days of the week, our hearts yield to hatred and deceit. The Sabbath is the actual product of what we do all the rest of the week. Religion is concerned not so much with what we do on one day, the Sabbath, as with what we do the other six days of the week. If we live worthily on the other six days, then it is far easier to keep the seventh day holy.

LEADERS MUST SET THE EXAMPLE

The chieftains brought onyx stones and other stones to be set for the ephod and for the breastplate (Exodus 35:27).

In Nahum Sokolov's book *L'maranan v'rabanan* "To the Rabbis," he pointed out how important it was for the Rabbis of Eastern Europe to go to Israel. When he asked Rabbi Shlomo David Kahana, formerly Chief Rabbi of Warsaw, to convene the Rabbis so that he might expound the *mitzvah* of settling in Israel, Rabbi Kahana said: "All the Rabbis love Israel. First call the people together and persuade them to go. You can always count on the Rabbis."

Nahum Sokolov replied: "Tradition tells us that when Moses asked the *Nesiim* 'the chieftains' of the tribes to make their contributions toward the erection of the Tabernacle, they said: 'We are ready to give. You can always count on us. Go to the people; let them give first.'

"Well, you know what happened," Sokolov said. "The people gave so much that Moses did not require the gifts of the chieftains. Therefore the *Nesiim* had no part in building the Tabernacle itself. But later they contributed "onyx stones and the stones to be set for the ephod and for the breastplate." The word *Nesiim* is written without a *yod* to indicate that there was something lacking in their character because they did not immediately respond to the appeal of Moses.

"You answer me as did the *Nesiim*," Sokolov continued. " 'Get the others first.' Wouldn't it be unfortunate if Palestine were to be built without these outstanding Rabbis?"

This actually happened. Because the great Rabbis of Poland and Russia did not go to Israel, the *yod*, symbol of a vital and dynamic Judaism, is still missing among many in Israel. There are many indications however, that Israel's religious life will again flourish in every part of the Land.

In Jewish community life throughout the world, the leaders should never say: "You can always depend on us; get the others first." The leaders must set the example.

OUR THREE NAMES

Moses said to the Children of Israel: "See, the Lord has called by name Bezalel, the son of Uri, the son of Hur, of the tribe of Judah" (Exodus 35:30).

Bezalel was a great artist. He was endowed by God with wisdom, understanding and knowledge of all manner of workmanship, to make designs for work in gold, silver, and brass, to cut stones for setting and to carve wood—to work in all manner of skillful workmanship (Exodus 35:31,32).

According to a Midrash, everyone has three names: the one his parents gave him, the one by which his friends call him, and the one which he makes for himself. The name given to Bezalel by his parents was Reaiah (I Chronicles 4:2; 5:5); his friends must have called him "the craftsman"; but God called him Bezalel which means "in the shadow of God." We can surmise that he made this name for himself because he was righteous and always in the presence (in the shadow) of God.

We do not choose the name our parents give us. Our friends often give us a nickname, but our real name we make for ourselves by the way we live.

LEADERS SHOULD RENDER
AN ACCOUNT OF STEWARDSHIP

These are the accounts of the Tabernacle as they were rendered according to the command of Moses . . . (Exodus 38:21).

The story is told of a prominent community leader who took offense when asked to give an account of the money he had collected. "Don't the people trust me?" he angrily demanded, and resigned his position as president. But because he was an exceptionally devoted worker, the committee asked the Rabbi to speak to him.

When the Rabbi asked him: "Are you superior to Moses?" the community leader replied: "Certainly not. Why do you ask?"

The Rabbi opened the Bible to Exodus 38:21 and read:

"These are the accounts of the Tabernacle as they were rendered according to the command of Moses, through the service of the Levites, by the hand of Ithamar, son of Aaron, the Priest." Then follows a detailed summary of the quantity of gold and brass used in constructing the Tabernacle.

The leader understood, withdrew his resignation, and rendered a detailed financial report.

Every leader is required to give an account of his stewardship, and this is never any reflection on his honor or integrity.

MOSES SET UP THE TABERNACLE

Moses set up the Tabernacle . . . (Exodus 40:18).

Moses did not actually build the Tabernacle. The work was
done by craftsmen under the direction of Bezalel, Ohaliab and
others. The Midrash relates however, that when the various
parts of the Tabernacle were completed, no one was able to
assemble them except Moses. This is to show that in all under-
takings, intelligence is as essential as physical strength; brain
is as important as brawn.

The Bible also gives other reasons why Moses is credited
with the setting up of the Tabernacle. He had planned the
work and therefore saw to it that everything was done according to divine command as revealed to him.

David is similarly credited with building the Temple. The
superscription of Psalm 30 reads: "A Song of David for the
dedication of the Temple." Why "A Song of David" in view
of the fact that Solomon actually built the Temple? Although
David was no longer alive when the Temple was built, it was
he who had implanted the idea and was devoted to it; therefore,
the Temple was called by his name.

We read in Psalm 132:1-5, "Lord, remember unto David all
his affliction; how he vowed unto the Lord, and unto the Mighty
One of Jacob: 'Surely I will not enter the tent of my house, nor
ascend the bed that is spread for me; I will not give sleep to my
eyes, nor slumber to my eyelids until I find a place for the Lord,
a dwelling place for the Mighty One of Jacob.' " Because David
envisioned it and was consecrated to its completion, he is given
credit for the building of the Temple.

Thus it was with Moses. The Bible tells us in Numbers 7:1:
"Moses completed the setting up of the Tabernacle." Because
Moses was so devoted to the idea of building the Tabernacle,
its erection is ascribed to him even though he did not do any
of the actual work in building it.

THE TORAH CARRIES US

Moses took the Testimony (Tablets of the Law) and placed it in the Ark . . . (Exodus 40:20).

Commenting on this verse, the exegetes tell us *Ha-aron nosay et nosov* "The Ark carried those who transported it." Based on this interpretation, others say: *Ha-Torah nosah et no-se-eha* "The Torah lifts those who hold it."

When an old man at a Sabbath service asked for the *mitzvah* of *hagbahah* "lifting the Torah Scroll," the sexton said: "This Torah is very heavy. I don't think you'll be able to lift it."

The old man replied: "I believe that when you lift the Torah, the Torah lifts you; yea, it uplifts and exalts you."

The story is told that when the Jews were herded into the Warsaw ghetto, they were warned that if they did not run they would be beaten. An old man, bent and infirm, was leading his grandchild by the hand. As they ran, the child fell and bruised his leg. When he arose he could only limp along. Fearing that the Nazis would club the boy, the old man placed him on his shoulder and forced himself to keep running.

"What are you doing?" someone asked. "You can hardly run yourself; you are old and weak. How can you carry the child on your shoulder?"

"How wrong you are!" the old man replied. "I am not carrying the child; the child is carrying me. Were it not for him, I would not be able to take a step."

When we uphold the teachings of the Torah or pursue any worthy goal or purpose, they sustain us; no task is too difficult or impossible.

ויקרא

The wilderness is shadowed in darkness; only the horizon reminds us of Sinai. Above, we see the thousands of tents of the Children of Israel. In the center of the scene, the Tabernacle radiates spiritual light that, bringing with it solidarity, purpose and divine guidance, seems to penetrate each tent. The Priests are the guardians of that light, and the flame on the altar suggests their uninterrupted, sacred service. The tall, bright column above the Tabernacle reminds us of the *Shekhinah,* the protective power of God.

And Moses said . . . . . . וַיֹּאמֶר מֹשֶׁה

unto Aaron: Draw . . . . . אֶל אַהֲרֹן

near unto the . . . . קְרַב אֶל

altar . . . . הַמִּזְבֵּחַ

9:7 ט׳ז

LEVITICUS

LEVITICUS 1:1 — 5:26

THE LITTLE LETTER, *ALEPH*

The Lord called to Moses . . . (Leviticus 1:1).

Aleph, the last letter in the first word of *Vayikra* which begins
the Book of Leviticus, is written in smaller script than the
other letters. Why is this? In ancient times, the Bible was written in one continuous script, with no space between words.
When the last letter of any word was the same as the first of the
following word (as we find here where *Vayikra* ends with an
aleph and is followed by a word which begins with an *aleph*),
one letter suffices for both. Later, when there was space left between words, both letters were written, but one was smaller, to
indicate that it was not originally in the text. This is the historical explanation.

There is also a mystical explanation for the use of the smaller
letter *aleph*. In ancient times, children invariably began their
study of the Bible with the Book of Leviticus. God is, of course,
the best teacher, but how can God teach little children? He
must use a small *aleph* so as to reach the level of the child's
perception.

One year, all the visitors to Mount Zion were invited to inscribe a letter in a new *Sefer Torah* which was then being completed there. It is considered a great *mitzvah* for every Jew to
write at least one letter on the parchment of a scroll of the
Torah. The Book of Leviticus was reserved for children so
that each one could write a letter in it. For that purpose, a
group of school children one day came to Mount Zion, but
among them was a woman who said to the Curator: "My son
is sick and unable to come. He is heart-broken and is crying
because he cannot inscribe one of the letters. Would it be possible for you to bring the Torah scroll to him?"

"I am sorry," said the Curator, "I cannot do that."

103

That night, he had a strange dream in which he saw all the letters of the alphabet dancing above his head. He was trying to catch the small *aleph,* but it always eluded him, and the Curator asked: "Why do you run away?"

"I will have nothing to do with you," replied the *aleph.* "I am the *aleph* of God who made me small so that I might teach little children. Today, you have refused a child the *mitzvah* of inscribing a letter in the Torah. You are in charge of Mount Zion, the Holy Mountain. But I can turn the whole mountain into nothing but dust and ashes."

Thereupon the little *aleph* blew one breath, and the mountain disappeared.

When the Curator awoke he was very disturbed. And instantly he understood the meaning of this strange dream. "Yes, it is true," he said. "That little *aleph* which was made to teach Torah to children is so powerful that it can destroy the Holy Mountain, yet I was unwilling to make it possible for a child to inscribe a letter in the scroll and carry out the *mitzvah:* 'He who writes one letter in the Torah is as meritorious as if he had written the entire Torah.'"

He realized at once what a mistake he had made, and that day, he himself carried the Torah scroll to the sick child so that he could inscribe therein his letter.

A LEADER'S WORK IS CONTINUOUS

The Lord called to Moses . . . (Leviticus 1:1).

Throughout the Book of Exodus, we find the expressions, "God *spoke* to Moses" and "God *said* to Moses." The Book of Leviticus, however, begins: "The Lord ~alled to Moses." Our sages point out that when God desires to manifest His love for someone, He *calls* him. Why was Moses *called?* And why did God hold this affection for him?

Moses had three tasks to perform: to lead the Israelites out of Egypt, to give them the Torah on Mount Sinai, and to build the Tabernacle. The Book of Exodus tells us how he performed these three *mitzvot*. With this three-fold mission completed, Moses thought he was no longer needed.

"I have led my people to freedom; I have transmitted to them God's Torah, and now that the spirit of God is present in the Tabernacle, my work is done," he said.

But God thought otherwise. He knew that He needed Moses more than ever before. And with great affection for Moses because of all he had accomplished, He *called* to Moses and said: "Now we have to teach the people the importance of ritual and the primacy of the moral laws, such as 'Love your neighbor as yourself' and others which are found in the Holiness Code, Leviticus, chapter 19. Until that is accomplished your work is not finished."

Thus it is that whenever a great spiritual leader completes one task, he must never cease to serve, because the inspiration of his spirit is essential to influence and stimulate others to continue his endeavors on behalf of mankind.

THE IMPORTANCE OF SACRIFICE

Speak to the Children of Israel and say to them: "When any man brings an offering . . ." (Leviticus 1:2).

The Book of Leviticus deals largely with the rites and specifications concerning those animal sacrifices which our ancestors brought to the Temple of God. In past ages, pagan nations brought sacrifices to their idols, but their sacrifices consisted not only of animals, but human beings, especially children. The Jews, however, obedient to the teachings of their Prophets, abhorred and condemned these inhuman practices and sacrificed only animals, birds, and measures of grain.

Some sacrifices were in thanksgiving to God for His many blessings, and some, as an atonement, asking God's forgiveness for their sins. In offering such sacrifices, our ancestors felt themselves closer to God. In fact, the Hebrew word *korban* is derived from the word which means "to come near." This stresses the important truth that, when we make sacrifices on behalf of our religion, we come closer to God.

God does not need sacrifices; but *man does*. Nineteen centuries ago, when the Temple at Jerusalem was destroyed, all animal sacrifices were abolished. Thereafter, in place of sacrifices, the Rabbis substituted prayer and good deeds, which invariably help to bring man closer to God.

Although we no longer offer animal sacrifices, we still believe in "making sacrifices." Indeed, nothing worth while is ever accomplished without some form of sacrifice. All the good things we enjoy are the result of sacrifice in one form or another. The freedom we possess, the books that instruct us, the medicines that heal us, the religion that sustains us—all of these have been achieved through sacrifice.

All around us, every day, sacrifices are being made. Parents are constantly sacrificing their own comfort and pleasure for the sake of their children. Students sacrifice precious time and energy in order to prepare for some worth while profession. Men and women even give up their lives for causes in which they profoundly believe. The best things in life carry the highest price-tags. It is certainly worth while to make sacrifices for all the things that to us are most precious and sacred: our ideals, our Torah, our children, our family, our people, our country.

THE SACRIFICE
WHICH GOD HOLDS MOST PRECIOUS

. . . The fire of the altar shall be kept burning on it (Leviticus 6:2).

Mystics tell us that whatever has been created shall forever exist. If this is true, where is the altar of the Temple which was destroyed almost 2000 years ago?

The altar is within every human heart. "The fire of the altar shall be kept burning on it." The Hebrew word *bo* in this verse can mean either "on it" or "in him." The mystics therefore declare that the fire of the altar shall be kept forever burning in the descendants of Aaron the High Priest and in all of us. They tell us that everyone is a Priest, every life is a Temple, and every human heart is an altar. Whenever our good inclinations prevail over our evil inclinations, we thereby bring a sacrifice upon the altar within us. Every good deed adds brilliance to the spiritual fire that burns in our hearts.

We are told that on one occasion the angels, wanting to find out what sacrifice is most precious to God, brought Him part of the uniform of a soldier who had given his life for his country. God said this was indeed a great sacrifice but He did not consider it to be the most precious.

The angels then brought Him the cap of a nurse who had tended a patient whom she knew was suffering from a contagious disease. She had contracted the disease and died. God said this was certainly a great sacrifice, but that He still did not regard it the most precious.

The angels then brought Him two small human tears. On beholding them, God said these tears were more precious to Him than any other sacrifice. But why? Who had shed them?

108

A man carrying a knife was seeking revenge on a friend who had maligned him. That night as he approached his former friend's house, he looked through the window and beheld his intended victim happily playing with his children and smiling at his lovely wife. At this sight his heart melted and the would-be murderer was so moved that he shed two tears, threw aside his knife and went away. And these were the tears that the angels had brought to God.

Whenever we overcome our own evil inclinations, we bring to God the sacrifice which He considers most precious of all.

EVERY USEFUL TASK IS HOLY

The Priest shall then take off his vestments and put on other vestments, and carry the ashes outside the camp to a clean place (Leviticus 6:4).

One day the *shamash* (sexton) of a *Beth Hamidrash* "a House of Study," was ill and confined to his bed. When the people came to worship in the *Beth Hamidrash,* they found it most untidy. The mud they had dragged in on their boots the previous day was still on the floor. The worshipers all complained, but not one of them thought of taking a broom and sweeping it up.

The Hasidic Rabbi decided to teach his congregation a lesson. He put on his holiday garments: his *kapote* "long cloak," and *shtreimel* "wide-brimmed hat," and took a broom to sweep the room.

His disciples were astonished. "What are you doing?" they asked.

"I am doing what the Priest did in the Tabernacle in the wilderness and in the Temple at Jerusalem," replied the Rabbi, and he quoted the above verse from Leviticus 6:4.

"In a House of God," he explained, "all labor is holy, even the most menial. The entire world is a Temple, and every task that is useful is holy."

THE COMPLETE DAY

*Fire shall be kept burning on the altar continually; it shall
not go out (Leviticus 6:6).*

According to the mystics, whatever was created shall forever
exist. "But how about the Temple?" we ask. And their answer
is that, although the physical building and all its stones and
timbers are gone, the meaning, purpose, functions, and the
pattern of service in the Temple still exist.

In the Temple, every morning and evening, a burnt offering,
constituting public sacrifice, was laid upon the altar. This "per-
petual offering" was called *Tamid.* We read in Leviticus 6:2,5
that the burnt offering must be kept burning throughout the
night, and that its flame must be used to kindle the wood for
the morning offering.

Since that day, prayer has been substituted for sacrifice. If we
begin our day with prayer, the entire day is likely to be filled
with the spirit of God. And our evening prayer makes the day
complete. For this reason, the tradition-revering Jew begins
every morning with the *Shema* (Deuteronomy 6:4-9) and ends
the day with the *Shema.* In this manner, the morning and evening prayers follow the pattern of service in the Temple of old.
When we address ourselves to our Heavenly Father every morning and evening, the spiritual fire shall burn on our altar continually and thus we are afforded the ever-renewed opportunity
of investing our life daily with reverence and purpose.

THE REPENTANT SINNER
SHALL NOT BE EMBARRASSED

. . . To the place where the burnt offering is brought, there shall the sin offering be brought (Leviticus 6:18).

Although, with the destruction of the Temple, the institution of sacrifice was abolished, certain moral lessons can still be drawn from the regulations concerning the offering of sacrifices.

If one had committed a sin and wanted to atone by bringing a sacrifice, he might well have hesitated because he would feel embarrassed. Those who would see him bringing a sin offering would at once know that he had sinned. But in the Temple at Jerusalem, to avoid any embarrassment, it was ordered that the sin offering should be made in the very same place as the free-will offering. Thus, no one would publicly be put to shame.

There are prayers which are to be said *b'lahash* "silently." In the weekday *Amidah*, one of the prayers to be said silently is the confession of sin and the purpose for this is that no one may be embarrassed to confess his sins. In the *Ethics of the Fathers*, we read: "He who publicly puts his fellow man to shame shall have no share in the world to come."

GOD'S HAND PROTECTS

Aaron raised his hands toward the people and blessed them
. . . (Leviticus 9:22).

In this verse, the Hebrew word for "hands" is written in the singular because one *yod* is missing. But the word is read as if it were in the plural. Our Rabbis say that since the word is written in the singular, it refers to the "Hand of God."

The "Hand of God" was seen in the liberation from Egyptian bondage. It was similarly evident in the recent Israeli War of Independence. We are told that when thousands of Jews were approaching Mount Zion on their pilgrimage celebrating the Festival of Shavuot, the Priests on top of the mountain stood ready to bless the people. But when the Arabs on the other side of Mount Zion saw so many Jews assembled, they thought that they were coming to take Mount Zion away from them. The Arab soldiers elevated their rifles and began shooting, but miraculously not one Jew was killed.

"It was the Hand of God," the mystics say. "When the Priests raised their hands to bless the people, in that very act the Hand of God was also lifted, diverting the Arab's fire from the mountain."

113

THE SIN OF SILENCE

*Nadav and Abihu . . . each offered before the Lord, strange
fire . . . which He had not commanded them (Leviticus 10:1).*

There is an old midrash that Job and Balaam were Pharaoh's
counsellors, and when Job heard that the brothers Nadav and
Abihu had been destroyed by fire (Leviticus 10:1,2) because
they brought "strange fire" before the Lord, his heart sank with
fear. Why?

Because he also heard that Nadav had said to Abihu: "Would
that Moses and Aaron should die so that we might take their
places," and when Nadav said this, Abihu was silent. Yet Abihu
also perished in the Lord's fire.

Job then recalled that he himself had been silent when
Pharaoh summoned his counsellors to decide how to deal with
the Hebrews who were becoming too numerous. Balaam had
advised that all the Hebrew male children be thrown into the
Nile and he, Job, had said nothing. At that time he had thought
there was nothing wrong in keeping silent. But now when he
heard that Abihu had perished in the Lord's fire because he
said nothing in protest against his brother's utterance, Job became terrified.

It is not enough that we ourselves are not guilty of wrong-
doing; it is our duty to protest against evil, and to do our utmost
to prevent it. On vital moral issues, we cannot remain neutral.
When evil is being planned or perpetrated, we cannot escape
our own responsibility by doing nothing. To see injustice done
without protesting against it is to participate in that very injustice.

In his catalogue of human failings, Dante reserves a special
place for those who, in moments of great moral crisis, maintain
their neutrality and silence.

When the Nazis began their destruction first of the Jews and then of the Catholics and Protestants, the world leaders kept silent. They too are therefore guilty. The Eichmann trial gave eloquent testimony to the fact that not Eichmann alone was on trial; the German people and humanity as a whole were on trial because they had done nothing to prevent the massacre of millions of innocent people.

"Those who appeased the dictator, those who wished to be innocent bystanders, those who closed their frontiers to the refugees, and those who merely remained silent, contributed in different degrees to the downfall of man and his conscience in the twentieth century."

We must ever remember the Biblical injunction: "You shall not stand idly by when the blood of your neighbor is spilled" (Leviticus 19:16).

TEACHING IS ONLY HALF THE TASK

Then Moses diligently inquired . . . (Leviticus 10:16).

Modern parents often complain that, though they do their utmost to teach their children high moral principles, young people of today will not listen. And teachers likewise deplore that, although they try to inculcate ethical standards and values, they can exert no influence upon the conduct of their pupils. Why is this so?

The answer is to be found in a significant interpretation of three words in the Bible—*Darosh darash Moshe:* "Moses diligently inquired." These three words happen to occur exactly in the middle of the Five Books of Moses. The first, *darosh,* ends the first half of the Pentateuch, and the second, *darash,* begins the second half.

Our sages say that the first word, *darosh,* means "to teach," which is only half the task of instructing mankind. The second, *darash,* means "to show by example." To exemplify what we say by what we do is the second half of the task. Teaching alone is never enough. Our own example must complete the task of instructing others, young or old, in the ways of right thinking and doing.

THE ART OF LISTENING

When Moses heard, he was well pleased (Leviticus 10:20).

One Sabbath, a Rabbi invited a visiting colleague to speak to his congregation. This Rabbi, extremely fatigued, was not in the mood to preach, yet he did not want to offend his friend. So he quoted the verse from Leviticus 10:20, and added: "Moses always taught and the people listened, but on this occasion Aaron spoke, and Moses listened and was well pleased. Since I am always speaking and teaching, I want now to hear what you have to say."

It is essential that we should cultivate the art of listening. Parents are continually talking to their children, and teachers are continually talking to their pupils, but there comes a time when we must listen to what our children and pupils say if we expect them to listen to us.

In his latter years, the Rabbi of Lubavitch was so ill that he could not speak above a whisper. Yet he continued to give lengthy lectures to his disciples, who crowded close so that they could hear his every word.

Once a famous preacher came to see the Rabbi of Lubavitch and when he heard the learned Rabbi talk in a whisper to his students and disciples, he was puzzled.

"I don't understand it," he said. "I have a booming baritone voice yet, if I speak more than half-an-hour, my congregation is bored and complains. Your Rabbi can scarcely speak above a whisper, yet all of you lean forward to catch every word and you listen to him for hours."

"Ah!" said one of the students. "We listen to him for hours because all of us know that if any one of us were to speak to the Rabbi for hours, he would lean forward in order to listen to us."

It is self-evident that only he who listens well can ever teach well.

DO NOT JUDGE BY APPEARANCE

When a man has on the skin of his body a swelling, a scab or a bright spot . . . (Leviticus 13:1).

The *Sidrah Tazria* speaks of scabs, boils, leprosy and other diseases of the skin. Why are these mentioned in the Bible? The obvious reason is the importance of hygiene and health. But there is another lesson we can learn from the story of Elazar ben Shimon.

Elazar was one day returning from Migdal Eder when he met a repellant-looking man with scabs on his face, who wanted to join him. Elazar turned away and muttered under his breath: "What an ugly man!" The man overheard him.

"Go! Tell it to the Creator," he said. "Ask Him why He made me so ugly."

Elazar instantly regretted his words and asked the stranger to forgive him. And thereafter he always taught his pupils that, when they would see anyone who was disfigured and repulsive, they should never turn away from him because he too is a child of God.

The Bible deals with the subject of scabs, boils and disease, in order to teach us not only the importance of cleanliness and hygiene, but also indirectly to point out that every human being is precious to God regardless of his appearance and that we must judge our fellow men by their character, not by their face.

A Roman princess was once much impressed by the wisdom of Rabbi Joshua who happened to be a hunchback.

"Why," she asked him, "did God pour so much wisdom into such an unattractive vessel?"

Rabbi Joshua replied with a question: "Where does your father, the King, keep his best wine?"

"In earthenware vessels," she answered.

"Poor people also keep their wine in earthenware vessels," said the Rabbi. "Your father is extremely wealthy. Why doesn't he keep his wine in vessels of gold and silver?"

The princess thereupon ordered her retainers to pour the wine from earthenware vessels into those of gold and silver. But when that wine was served at a banquet it was sour. The King was furious until he heard the story from the princess.

"Don't you know," he asked her, "that wine keeps best in earthenware vessels?"

Perhaps this parable explains why God gives wisdom not necessarily to the most beautiful people, but very often to those who are physically unattractive.

SEE YOURSELF IN OTHERS

The Priest shall examine the plague . . . and pronounce him unclean (Leviticus 13:3).

The Priests were in those days the first diagnosticians and physicians. But the Kabalists interpret this verse in a metaphysical sense.

They say that a wealthy Hasid once complained to his Rabbi that he was annoyed by a certain man who, along with others, visited his home for the Sabbath afternoon gathering.

"He is vain and conceited," declared this Hasid. But the Rabbi reproved him.

"Look at yourself. Perhaps *you* are vain and conceited."

"What do you mean?" asked the Hasid, and the Rabbi explained:

"In the Temple of old, there was a special mirror and, when anyone looked into it he saw not only his physical appearance but also all the good and the evil in himself. But now that the Temple no longer exists, the Kabalists say that every man is a mirror. What one man sees in such a mirror is likely to be a reflection of himself. If others appear to be wicked, he should look to himself; perhaps he also is wicked. If others appear to be good, that may indicate that there is good in him.

The Bible says that a man with a disease shall come to the Priest. According to these Kabalists, this also applies to the Priest who, while examining others, should also examine his own conduct to determine if there is any defect in himself.

When a leader finds a fault in his people, the fault may really be in him.

GOD'S PRESENCE BRINGS PEACE

The owner of the house shall come and tell the Priest: "It appears to me as if a plague were in my house!" (Leviticus 14:35).

A discontented and restless man once complained to his Rabbi: "I don't know why there is no peace in my home. Everyone is constantly quarreling. It appears to me as if there were a *nega* 'a plague,' on my house."

The Rabbi pointed out that the expression *nireh li*, "It appears to me," occurs only twice in the Bible, once in connection with the plague (Leviticus 14:35) and once in the Book of Jeremiah: "The Lord appeared to me from afar" (31:3). Although the meaning in the verse from Jeremiah is different from that of the one in Leviticus, the fact that in each, the same Hebrew phrase *nireh li* is used, lends itself to a homiletical interpretation.

"You feel as if there were a plague on your home. Perhaps it is because God is far away," the Rabbi said. "It may be that you have not invited God into your home. Wherever there is the spirit of God, there also is the love of family and *shalom bayit* 'a peaceful home.' When God's presence is in your home, the letters *nun gimel* and *ayin* which spell the word *nega* 'plague' will be transposed into the letters *ayin nun gimel*, and thus form the word *oneg* 'joy.' "

The man took this to heart and later reported to his Rabbi:

"I took your advice. Religion at last plays a vital role in our home, and now there is harmony and contentment. Now I understand the meaning of the Psalm: 'Except the Lord builds the house, they labor in vain who build it' " (127:1).

SEEDS OF WISDOM TAKE ROOT

This is the law . . . to teach concerning the clean and un-clean (Leviticus 14:54,57).

On one occasion a student criticized his master. "You spend all your time teaching, but there are many who do not listen. And some of your listeners are not even believers. How can you ever teach such people?"

In reply the Rabbi quoted this verse from Leviticus 14:57: "This is the law to teach concerning all manner of disease, concerning the clean and the unclean."

"This last phrase," he said, "is usually interpreted as an injunction to give instruction concerning the laws of cleanliness and uncleanliness, but it also has a more profound meaning. It refers not to laws, but also to people, some of whom are said to be 'clean' and some 'unclean.' It therefore implies that we are to teach both the 'clean' (the believers) and the 'unclean' (the nonbelievers): i.e., those who are willing to learn, and those who are unwilling and unreceptive.

"Moses graphically compared the Torah to rain (Deuteronomy 32:2) because, when the rain falls upon the earth, it turns to mud, which is 'unclean.' But in the mud, seeds often germinate, and green plants and flowers spring forth. Likewise, if we persist in teaching, the seeds of our teaching may in time germinate even in the 'unclean' and then come to fruition."

THE BUILDERS OF ZION

In this manner shall only Aaron enter the holy place . . .
(Leviticus 16:3).

The late Chief Rabbi Abraham Kook was a great friend of
the *halutzim,* those pioneers who were reviving the land of
Palestine and were making the desert bloom. One of the Rabbi's
intimate friends was critical of this.

"I am surprised that you're so friendly with these *halutzim,*"
he remarked. "They're so irreligious. They don't observe the
Sabbath. They don't even *layg t'fillin* (put on the phylacteries)."

"They may not *layg t'fillin,*" replied the Rabbi, "but they do
layg tzigel. They may not put on phylacteries but they do lay
bricks. And the time will yet come when these *halutzim* will
truly observe our religious practices. From the Bible we learn
that no one was allowed to enter the Holy of Holies except the
High Priest, and then only once a year. But even he could not
enter, except in a carefully prescribed manner. *B'zot yavo* 'In
this manner shall he enter' . . . (Leviticus 16:3).

"But you may ask, as did the sages: 'Suppose there was a leak
in the roof or a wall was weakened, could not workmen enter
the Holy of Holies?' The answer was: 'Of course. The law does
not apply to those who build and repair.'

"In like manner," Rabbi Kook continued, "we are now in the
process of restoring our ancient homeland. These *halutzim* are
now the builders. When our homeland will be rebuilt, they
too shall observe our religious traditions."

EVERY JEW A HIGH PRIEST

In this manner shall only Aaron (the High Priest) enter the holy place . . . (Leviticus 16:3).

None but the High Priest could enter the Holy of Holies, and even he only once a year, and then only in accordance with certain prescribed regulations. The Bible uses the expression: *B'zot yavo* "In this manner shall he enter (Leviticus 16:3). The numerical value of the letters *zayin, aleph,* and *tav* in the word *b'zot* is 408.

In the High Holiday prayers we read: Repentance, Prayer and Deeds of Kindness annul the severity of judgment." In the old editions, the Hebrew word *tzom* "fasting" appears in small letters directly above the word *Teshuvah* "Repentance"; the word *kol* "voice" appears above the word *Tefillah* "Prayer"; and the word *mammon* "money" appears above the word *Tzedakah* "Deeds of Kindness." *

The numerical value of each of the three words, *tzom, kol,* and *mammon* is 136. All three are thus equal, and this symbolizes that man needs all three. The combined numerical value of the three words, *tzom, kol,* and *mammon* is 408. And the numerical value of the word *b'zot* "in this manner" is also 408. This indicates that the High Priest could procure atonement for his people only if he practiced all three principles: repentance, prayer and deeds of kindness.

Since the Temple was destroyed, and there is no longer a High Priest, every Jew must consider himself a High Priest, in accordance with the Biblical declaration: "You shall be unto Me a Kingdom of Priests and a holy people" (Exodus 19:6).

---

* See page 37.

BEGIN WITH YOURSELF

. . . When Aaron has made atonement for himself, for his household, and for the entire assembly of Israel . . . (Leviticus 16:17).

Before the Rabbi of Meseritz died, he bequeathed the following to his disciples: to one he gave his good health; to another, his wisdom; and to a third, his sense of humor. But to Rabbi Elimelekh of Lizensk, he entrusted the task of *tikun haolam* "of improving the world."

When the Rabbi of Meseritz died, Rabbi Elimelekh went out into the world to work among the people and try to improve their way of life. At the end of two years, he returned home and, one day while lying on his couch, he began pondering: "Have I succeeded? Are the people any better now than they were?" To his sorrow, he felt constrained to answer "No."

Then, falling asleep, he dreamt that he was complaining to his master, the deceased Rabbi of Meseritz:

"Your other disciples," he said, "have all succeeded, but why have I not succeeded?" And in his dream he heard his master reply:

"It's true, you went out into the world in order to make people better, but what about the people in your own city of Lizensk?"

Rabbi Elimelekh took this rebuke to heart and began working with the people of his own city. But after a few months, one day as he lay on his couch, he fell again to pondering: "Have I," he asked himself, "succeeded with the people of my own city?" Again he was forced to answer "No." And he dreamt that once more he was communing with his departed master.

"You tried to improve the people of your city," said the master, "but how about those in your home: your own wife, children and grandchildren?"

After several months of attempting to correct the faults of his own family, Rabbi Elimelekh once more fell to self-questioning.

"Have I," he wondered, "succeeded with the members of my own household?" And alas, he had to admit that the answer was "No." Finally, the Rabbi of Meseritz appeared as in previous dreams and Rabbi Elimelekh, discouraged, told him he had failed in his mission.

"What about yourself?" asked the Rabbi of Meseritz. "Have you begun with yourself?"

From this it appears that the only way to help others to mend their ways is to begin with ourselves. Thus the Bible records that the High Priest first made atonement for himself, then for his household, and finally for the entire assembly of Israel (Leviticus 16:17).

THE VALUE OF LAWS IN THE NEGATIVE

. . . Do not follow the practices of the land of Egypt where you dwelt, nor those of the land of Canaan to which I shall bring you; nor shall you follow their customs (Leviticus 18:3).

Why is this command formulated in the negative? There is this story which gives us the answer.

A certain man was lost in a great forest and could not find his way out. By chance he met another wayfarer and spoke to him.

"I am certainly relieved to find someone else in these woods. Can you please tell me how to get out of here?"

"I'm sorry," replied the stranger, "but I too am lost. I can't tell you the way out, but I can tell you where *not* to go." Pointing to several trails, he said: "I've gone in this direction and in that, but I can tell you not to take those paths. They will not lead you out of the woods."

The Children of Israel were told whom *not* to follow and where *not* to go if they were to remain loyal to God. Thus it is frequently essential to be told what not to do, and therefore many of our laws, ordinances, rules and regulations are expressed in negative terms. Half of the Ten Commandments and 365 of the 613 *mitzvot* are prescribed in the negative.

YOU LOVE GOD WHEN YOU LOVE
YOUR FELLOW MAN

. . . You shall love your neighbor as yourself; I am the Lord (Leviticus 19:18).

Philosophers and theologians have always disputed as to which should be more greatly stressed: the love of God or the love of man. Some say that if you teach man to love God, he will love his fellow man. Others say that if you teach man to love his fellow man, he will also love God. Only once does the Bible tell us "to love God" (Deuteronomy 6:5), but to "love our fellow man" is mentioned twice (Leviticus 19:18,34). This would seem to indicate that the love of man is a prerequisite to the love of God.

A man by the name of Judah said to his Rabbi: "I notice that all our *b'rakhot* (blessings) are expressed in the plural and that every Jew, before he puts on his *tallit* (prayer shawl), still recites the *b'rakhot* in the plural and says: 'Praised art Thou, O Lord our God, King of the universe, who hast given *us* the *mitzvah* of the *tallit*.' If this is a personal prayer, why is it expressed in the plural?"

"The blessing is in the plural," replied the Rabbi, "in order to indicate that one cannot live unto himself alone, that he is a part of the community and should therefore think not only of himself when he prays, but also of his fellow men and their well being. Before you can approach God through prayer, you must show your love and concern for your fellow man. Thus Ari (Rabbi Isaac Lurie) and his disciples always used to dispense charity to the needy before commencing their morning prayer which they always began with the verse, 'Love your neighbor as yourself.' They felt that they had no right to approach God without first expressing their love and compassion for their fellow man."

DO NOT BEAR A GRUDGE

You shall not take vengeance, nor bear a grudge against the
children of your people . . . (Leviticus 19:18).

On one occasion Hayim asked his Rabbi why he showed so
much respect for a certain visitor, Mordecai. When the Rabbi
replied: "He was a great scholar," Hayim expressed surprise.

"When I talked with Mordecai, I did not hear from his lips
any words of wisdom."

The Rabbi explained that until recently Mordecai had always had a remarkable memory and never forgot anything that
he saw or heard. But one day a neighbor publicly insulted him.
Mordecai, a devout and pious man, forgave his neighbor and
tried to forget the whole incident. But, because he had such a
remarkable memory, he could not forget the humiliation his
neighbor had caused him.

He was so anxious to carry out the Biblical injunction never
to bear a grudge that he prayed God to take away his memory,
and his request was granted. "That's why nowadays," said the
Rabbi, "his conversation never reveals his scholarship." There
was a twinkle in his eye as the Rabbi went on:

"But in heaven, I am sure the angels will frequently consult
him on difficult matters."

WHERE THERE IS LOVE, THERE IS GOD

. . . You shall love your neighbor as yourself: I am the Lord (*Leviticus 19:18*).

When Rabbi Ruzhin was asked: "What is the connection between the command, 'You shall love your neighbor as yourself' and the words 'I am the Lord'?" he replied: "This means that God knows whether or not your love is genuine and when it is genuine, His Presence is with you."

In illustration of this, there is the story of two extremely devoted friends, Berel and Moshe, who were closer than brothers. One day Berel falsely accused of stealing the King's seal was sentenced to twenty years in prison. Moshe immediately sought an audience with the King.

"Your Majesty," he said, "my friend Berel did not steal your great seal. I stole it. Send *me* to prison."

The wise King instantly realized the great love Moshe had for Berel inasmuch as he offered to take this punishment in place of his friend, and he said: "Now I understand why the words 'I am the Lord' come after the phrase 'Love your neighbor as yourself.' Surely God is present when there is such love."

Whenever two people are devoted to each other, God is always with them. *Yod* is a Hebrew letter, and a Jew is often called a *Yud*. When two *yods* are written together, it is the abbreviation of God's name. When two *yuds* (Jews) are close together, God is there. But when two *yuds* are separated because of dissension, God is not there. And this applies to all peoples and all nations.

RESPECT OLD AGE

You shall rise before the hoary head and respect old age . . .
(Leviticus 19:32).

When Shmuel asked a certain Rabbi what he had that day
taught his pupils, the Rabbi replied:
"I explained the verse 'You shall rise before the hoary head
and respect old age.' "
Then Shmuel went to the Rabbi's pupils and questioned
them as to what they had learned that day.
"Our Rabbi taught us how we should live," they replied.
Returning to the Rabbi, Shmuel said: "You tell me one thing
and your students tell me another. Whom shall I believe?"
"This verse," explained the Rabbi, "means that we are to
revere not only the elders but also our own old age. We are
to live in such manner that, when we reach old age, we shall
have self respect and have earned the respect of others. *Ashray
yaldutenu shelo bishah et ziknatenu* 'Happy is our youth which
will not bring shame to our old age.' "

LEADERS MUST HAVE PUBLIC SUPPORT

*You shall sanctify them (the Priests); . . . they shall be holy
to you, for I the Lord who sanctifies you, am holy (Leviticus
21:8).*

The question may be asked why is it necessary for the people
to sanctify the Priests. Do Priests require sanctification by man?
Is it not sufficient that the Lord sanctifies them? It is explicitly
stated in the same *Sidrah* 21:23, "For I am the Lord who sanctifies them."

It is not enough that the Priests be sanctified only from on
high; they must be sanctified by the people as well. Neither a
Priest nor any other leader will exert much influence if he is
not held in esteem by the people whom he serves and guides.

Tradition relates that though Reuben was the first-born of
Jacob's sons, he forfeited his claim to the birthright; Jacob gave
it instead to Joseph. We should therefore expect that the leadership of the tribes of Israel would have passed down to Joseph's
descendants, especially since we are told that Jacob had trained
Joseph for leadership and Joseph had shown himself deserving.
Despite this, Judah and not Joseph was chosen to be head of the
people. "For Judah prevailed above his brethren, and of him
came he that is the prince; yet the birthright was Joseph's" (1
Chronicles 5:2).

The reason Judah became leader was because his brothers
acclaimed him their leader. He was recognized and accepted
by the people: "You, Judah, shall your brothers praise (recognize). Your father's sons shall bow down before you" (Genesis
49:8).

Titles and illustrious parentage are of little value for public
leaders if they do not have the support of the people they represent and lead.

132

HOW TO MEASURE A GIFT

. . . You shall bring an omer, the first sheaf of your harvest to the Priest (Leviticus 23:10).

We are told in mystic literature that, in return for bringing a sacrifice of the *omer,* the first sheaf of barley of the harvest, God promised Abraham that his descendants would enter the Holy Land. To us in the twentieth century, the offering of an *omer* may seem too insignificant to merit such a reward. But in the eyes of God, it is not *what* the sacrifice is, but *how* we bring it. The size of the gift does not matter so long as it comes from the heart.

There is an old folk tale that an astrologer once foretold that a certain Simon, while working with Zev in the forest, would that day be killed. But late that afternoon, both came home alive. When the astrologer saw that his prediction had not been fulfilled, he was surprised and asked that they tell him all that had happened that day. And Simon told him:

"We were both working until noonday, and then we sat down to eat. Zev forgot his lunch, and so I shared my bread with him."

"Where were you sitting when you ate your lunch?" asked the astrologer.

"On a bench under a tree," replied Simon.

"Take me to that bench," said the astrologer. And Simon led him to the very place where he and Zev had eaten their lunch.

The astrologer looked down, and there on the ground, tightly coiled, was a poisonous snake.

"There, you see," said the astrologer. "That snake was destined to kill you, Simon, but what can I do when your God is satisfied with a piece of bread? God has spared your life because you were compassionate and shared your bread with Zev."

God said to the Israelites in the wilderness: "I provided for each of you a portion of manna every day for forty years. All that I ask in return, to show your love and faith in Me, is that you bring Me a sheaf of barley one day every year."

Even a sheaf of grain is a fitting sacrifice if it is a gift that we offer with all our hearts.

HOW TO COUNT OUR YEARS

The Lord spoke to Moses on Mount Sinai: "Speak to the Children of Israel and say . . . 'Six years shall you sow your field, and six years shall you prune your vineyard and gather in the produce thereof. But in the seventh year, the land shall have a Sabbath of complete rest, a Sabbath to the Lord. You shall neither sow your field nor prune your vineyard' " (*Leviticus 25:1-4*).

Why does the Bible single out the law of the "Sabbatical Year" as having been promulgated on Mount Sinai where the Ten Commandments were given? Rashi, the great commentator, gives the traditional view: Just as all the stipulations of the law concerning the Sabbatical Year came from Mount Sinai, so do all the other laws in the Bible.

The Sabbatical Year proclaimed on Mount Sinai is symbolic of how we should estimate our length of days. On one occasion, when a student read in the *Ethics of the Fathers:* "The day is short; the work is great," he commented: "I am only twenty-one. I hope to live until seventy. In the forty-nine years to come, I shall have forty-nine times 365 days in each year, totalling 17,885 days. And since each day has twenty-four hours and every hour, sixty minutes, I shall have plenty of time."

Thereupon his teacher corrected his thinking:

"You are measuring life in terms of single years of 365 days each, but there is a far better way of reckoning the years of our life. We should count them in terms of Sabbatical periods of seven years each. The Ten Commandments which were given on Sinai where the Sabbatical Year was also proclaimed, suggest that man's span of life normally consists of ten Sabbatical periods of seven years each. You are twenty-one, and this means that you have already lived three Sabbatical periods. Instead of saying that you have forty-nine years ahead of you, you should say that you have only seven more Sabbatical periods to live. And so you see, the days of your life are all too short. You will better appreciate how precious is time when you think of life in terms of Sabbatical periods and not of one year at a time."

STRANGERS FIND EACH OTHER

. . . The land is Mine; you are but strangers and settlers with Me (Leviticus 25:23).

One of our sages explains this verse to mean that God says: "If you consider yourself a settler so that you have no need of Me and no need for religion, then I am a stranger to you. On the other hand, if you consider yourself a stranger, then I am a settler and I will encourage and aid you."

Strangers somehow find each other. Two Americans, on meeting for the first time in a foreign country, soon become friends. In this country they might have lived for years on the same street without ever having spoken to each other. But as strangers in another land, they are generally attracted to one another.

One member of a congregation was explaining to his Rabbi how he felt about his religion.

"I have been away from religion for a long time," he said. "You ask me how did I ever return to God? It was this way: all those years I felt like a stranger, but in my loneliness I found God, who is also alone. As the Psalmist (39:13) phrased it: 'Hear my prayer, O Lord, for I am a stranger with Thee . . .'"

When does a man feel that he is a stranger in this world? When he has lofty ideals to which the whole world seems indifferent, and people everywhere ignore and debase morality, truth and justice. Even in that hour of his loneliness, when man feels himself estranged and alone, he can indeed find God.

THE SWORD AND THE BOOK

But you will not hearken to Me and will not observe these commandments . . . (Leviticus 26:14-46).

The Midrash tells us: *Safra v'saifa yardu k'rukhim yahad* "The book and the sword came down from Sinai bound together." The people beheld the Book, the Torah, but no one saw the sword. This is sometimes interpreted to mean that on Mount Sinai, God proclaimed the commandments and at the same time uttered the punishments for those who break them. The punishments are all set forth in Leviticus 26:14-46. If the people will accept the *mitzvot,* all will be well with them. If not, "the sword"—misery, war, and destruction—will be visited upon them.

Another explanation is offered in the legend about King David who, it is said, would not accept the gift of a sword sent to him by a foreign ruler.

"I rely," David declared, "upon the blessing which Judah received from my ancestor, Jacob. That blessing is set forth in Genesis 49:8-12, and in those five verses the Hebrew letter *zayin* does not once appear. The letter *zayin* is shaped like a sword; and the word *zayin* means 'weapon.'

"My weapon shall be justice and not the sword," said David, the King.

THE VIRTUE OF THE THREE PATRIARCHS

Then will I remember My covenant with Jacob, also My covenant with Isaac and also My covenant with Abraham will I remember; and I will remember the land (Leviticus 26:42).

In the Prayer Book and in historical works, the names of the patriarchs always appear in their chronological order. Why in this passage are they mentioned in the reverse order?

Each of the three patriarchs was characterized by his own particular virtue: Abraham, by his lovingkindness; Isaac, by his reverence and piety; and Jacob, by his learning. Thus we read in Micah 7:20: "Thou wilt show truth (Torah) to Jacob and lovingkindness to Abraham" and in Genesis 31:53: "And Jacob swore by the reverence of his father Isaac."

According to an ancient legend, there was the hope that when the time would come for Israel's redemption, the Jews would return to Zion because they would possess "the virtue of Jacob," their love of Torah or learning. That is why Jacob's name was mentioned first in the above verse from Leviticus. Should the Jews not possess the virtue of Jacob, then they might possess the virtue of Isaac, which is piety. If this were still not present within them, they would return to Zion because of the virtue of Abraham which is lovingkindness.

So it was. When the State of Israel was established, all Jews did not possess Jacob's virtue of learning. There were no great scholars like Rashi, Maimonides or the Gaon of Wilna; nor were there outstanding saints like the Baal Shem Tov, Israel Salanter or Yitzhak Levi of Berditchev. On the contrary, the Jews of our generation privileged to witness the return to Zion, are noted not especially for their Torah (Jacob's virtue), or for their piety (Isaac's virtue), but for their lovingkindness, their generosity and philanthropy (Abraham's virtue).

The unprecedented growth and development of Israel are due in large measure to the generous response, support and gifts of Jews all over the world who are thus manifesting the virtue of Abraham, the prime exemplar of generosity and lovingkindness.

But it is not enough to have Abraham's virtue alone. For its further spiritual growth and greatness as a nation and "as a light to the world," the State of Israel now requires in addition, the virtue of Isaac, piety, reverence for God; and the virtue of Jacob, love of Torah. When the virtues of all three great patriarchs are manifested in Israel, and among the Jews throughout the world, then the last clause of our text shall also be fulfilled: "And God said: 'I will remember the land.' "

בְּמִדְבַּר

At the bottom of the picture, darkness floods the deep wadis found in many parts of the Holy Land. Should there be a sudden, heavy downpour in the wadi, no one could escape alive, and this is but one of the many dangers to be encountered. The luscious fruit of the Land of Milk and Honey is being carried on the shoulders of those sent to explore the land of Canaan. Nevertheless, doubt lingers in the hearts of most of the Children of Israel that they will ever possess it.

The Israelites' camp is far beyond in the mountains. Seldom does the *Shekhinah* or the rays of the sun enter the wadi. The mission of the twelve men to explore Canaan has been a test of their courage. All of them are chieftains, but only one has been found worthy to lead the Children of Israel into the Holy Land.

And they returned . . . . . וַיָּשֻׁבוּ מִתּוּר

from spying out the . . . . . הָאָרֶץ מִקֵּץ

land at the end of . . . . . . אַרְבָּעִים יוֹם

forty days . . . .

13:25   יג כה

NUMBERS

INHERIT AND BEQUEATH

Take a census of the entire community of the Children of Israel by their families, by their households . . . You shall have with you a man of every tribe; he shall be the head of his father's house (Numbers 1:2,4).

Jewish tradition permits anyone well versed in prayer to lead the Synagogue Service. In the Synagogue on Mount Zion, two men were arguing because each wanted to officiate. One was Shabatai, a native Israeli, and the other was Moshe, a newcomer.

"Who are you that you should officiate?" asked Moshe, the newcomer.

"I am of the sixth generation born in this country," Shabatai replied, and asked: "Who are you?"

"Although I have just arrived, I am the forerunner of a hundred generations who shall live here," said Moshe. "You represent the past, but I represent the future. I should have the honor of officiating."

They brought their dispute to the Rabbi who referred them to the Biblical text: "God told Moses: 'Take a census of the entire community of the Children of Israel, by their families, by their households . . . You shall have with you a man of every tribe; *he* shall be the head of his father's house' " (Numbers 1:2,4).

The word *hu* "he" which in Hebrew ends this verse, seems superfluous but it emphasizes that *he,* everyone in turn, should become the head of a household and should father a new generation.

The Rabbi accordingly decided that the newcomer was entitled to officiate. He explained that it is good to be proud of one's ancestors because there is a certain *yihus* "prestige" in being native-born of the sixth generation, but that is not enough. One must not only be a descendant; he must also become an ancestor. It is not enough to be guardians of the old; we must also be builders of the new. We must not only inherit, we must also bequeath. We can pay our debt to the past by so living that the future will be in debt to us.

LOOK BACK TO GO FORWARD

Now those that encamp on the east side toward the dawn,
shall be of the standard of the camp of Judah . . . (Numbers
2:3).

The "east side" and the "dawn" are the same. Both *kedmah*
and *mizrahah* mean "east." The Bible is never redundant, and
every word is meaningful. Then why does it use two expressions
to designate the same thing? Judah was encamped in the east.
But when his tribe marched onward they had to walk backwards, facing the Holy Ark, because it was irreverent to turn
one's back to it. Thus they advanced by walking backwards!

It was not easy to march backwards, and the tribe of Judah
would have preferred to change positions with another tribe.
But they knew their position was in the east especially since
the east was twice indicated. There is a legend that one of the
wise men in their ranks declared:

"We are of the tribe of Judah, the leader of all the tribes!
Although we walk backwards facing the Holy Ark, we nevertheless advance forward. Progress is frequently made by looking
back, facing our past."

In this manner must we advance. Oarsmen, rowing a boat, do
not face the direction in which they are going but the direction
from which they are coming. We, too, must know whence we
came in order to know whither we are going. We must face the
Holy Ark and learn from the teachings of our Prophets and
sages, in order to advance and shape our future.

WHAT WE GIVE AWAY IS OURS

Every man's sacred offering shall be his . . . (Numbers 5:10).

Yosef, a generous man, supported every good cause. But one day, when he donated an exceptionally large sum to an institution of learning, his children objected.

"You are giving too much away!" they complained. "If you go on like this, you will be penniless." But Yosef disagreed.

"On the contrary, whatever I give away is really mine," he said. "I have no concern with what I shall leave behind. When I come to heaven, I can bring only what I have given away. I can't take anything with me. I learned this from the Bible: 'Every man's sacred offering shall be his; whatsoever a man gives the Priests, it shall be his'   (Numbers 5:10).

"It should be noted that the phrase 'it shall be his' is repeated, and this teaches a great truth. What we give away on earth becomes ours in eternity; and what we give to God becomes truly ours."

The story is told of a society woman who died and, while being escorted to her permanent home in heaven, saw a beautiful mansion.

"Whose home is that?" she inquired. When the angel told her whose home it was, the woman exclaimed: "On earth, that man was my gardener! If he has such a magnificent home, I can imagine what mine will be like."

They passed many smaller homes and, entering a little street, paused before a house that was not even finished. There was only the floor, but no walls and no roof.

"Madam, this is your home," said the angel, "and here you are to live."

"What!" the woman exclaimed. "Surely you are mistaken. On earth, I had a gorgeous home; I entertained lavishly; I was very prominent. I can't live here!"

"I'm sorry, Madam," said the angel, "but this is all the material you sent here."

146

THE SIXTY LETTERS OF THE
THREE-FOLD BLESSING

The Lord bless you and keep you . . . *(Numbers 6:24).*

There is a legend that when he became King, Solomon was possessed by an overwhelming fear. He could not sleep, and every night was tormented by nightmares. His court physician prescribed various sleeping potions, but they did not help. One night, in desperation, he called upon the Prophet Nathan, who assured him that God would send sixty heroes who would certainly rid him of all his enemies so that he need no longer have any fear.

"That won't do any good," said Solomon. "Last night I dreamt about those heroes. I dreamt that sixty armed guards were placed around my bed . . . 'three score mighty men of the heroes of Israel, each armed with a sword, all expert in war; every man with his sword on his side because of fear in the night' (Song of Songs 3:7,8). I did not sleep all night. The presence of soldiers can never bring peace to my mind."

"Ah!" said the Prophet, "Those were not the heroes I refer to. The sixty heroes whom God will send to protect you are not men, but rather the sixty Hebrew letters in the Priestly Blessing: 'The Lord bless and keep you; the Lord make His spirit shine upon you and be gracious unto you. The Lord lift up His spirit unto you and give you peace' " (Numbers 6:24-26).

On hearing this, Solomon at once felt at ease. That night and every night thereafter, he slept soundly; his nightmares ceased, and he was no longer fearful of anything.

AFTER A CLIMAX OFTEN COMES A BRIEF DECLINE

It came to pass on the day when Moses completed setting up the Tabernacle, and had anointed and consecrated it . . . (Numbers 7:1).

The verse begins with the word *Va'yehi* "It came to pass." Our commentators tell us that, whenever the word *va'yehi* occurs at the beginning of a passage, it implies that there was trouble and sadness. What sadness could there have been on the day when Moses completed the erection of the Tabernacle? Should it not have been a day of rejoicing? Who could be sad?

According to legend, the Torah was seen standing in a corner in the Tabernacle and weeping, and Moses asked: "Why are you weeping? You should rejoice and be glad. We shall soon enter the Promised Land. There are *mitzvot ha'tluyot baaretz* 'special laws to be observed only in the Holy Land.'" The Torah answered: "Yes, but when the people enter the Holy Land, they will all be so busy getting settled and building their homes that they will forget all about me."

Everyone who visits the State of Israel nowadays is thrilled by the country's phenomenal material and physical achievements, but some are disappointed when they observe laxity in religious observance, especially on the part of the young. Nevertheless, we should remember that, after a climax, there is invariably a decline. After the creation of the world, there were the "fallen angels"; after the Garden of Eden, the disobedience of Adam and Eve; and after Moses had set up the Tabernacle, there was also a decline.

In our personal lives, after a wedding or some other significant milestone, there is usually a letdown.

But we must never be downhearted or discouraged. According to the mystics, *Yerida tzarikh aliyah* "A descent calls for an ascent." They meant that a man's soul descends to earth for the purpose of ascending to heaven. Man's goal in life is to grow spiritually, to improve and elevate himself, to reach great heights. Religious observance in Israel has not yet measured up to our expectations but once the hundreds of thousands of new immigrants are settled, the Torah shall go forth out of Zion and the word of God from Jerusalem.

THE LIGHT MUST SHINE OUT

The Lord spoke to Moses saying: "Speak to Aaron and say to him: 'When you go up to light the lamps . . .'" (Numbers 8:2).

There is an old legend that when the building plans of the Temple at Jerusalem were sent to King Hiram of Tyre, who furnished Solomon with the artists and builders, Hiram was greatly amused. Solomon's architects had indicated that the windows placed within the thick walls of the Temple were to be large on the outside and to gradually decrease in size until they became narrow on the inside.

Hiram returned the plans with the notation: "In order to bring maximum light into the Temple, it is necessary that the opening should be small on the outside but large inside. I would suggest that you correct these specifications."

But Solomon's architects returned the plans without any alterations. "The windows are not designed to bring into the Temple the light from outside," they explained. "The House of God needs no light from the outside. The windows are designed to beam the light *mibifnim hahutzah* from within the Temple to the world outside. That light is to radiate to all the four corners of the Holy Land."

The light and inspiration we receive in our Houses of God today should shine out far and wide and illuminate every area of man's endeavor so that religion may penetrate the hearts and lives of all people everywhere.

CLEANING AND LIGHTING THE LAMPS

The Lord spoke to Moses, saying: "Speak to Aaron, and say to him: 'When you go up to light the lamps, the seven lamps shall throw their light toward the menorah' " (Numbers 8:2).

The Midrash tells us that when the Tabernacle was completed, Moses and the Children of Israel rejoiced, but Aaron, the High Priest, was unhappy. Why? When Aaron saw the lavish gifts which the chieftains had contributed to the Tabernacle, his heart was sad because he had no precious gifts to offer. Thereupon God reassured him: "Your part is more glorious than theirs, for you will light the menorah."

But when Aaron learned that his task was also to clean the lamps before he kindled the light, he was aggrieved and said: "You don't need a Priest to cleanse the lamps; anyone can do that. Is that such a great privilege?"

Then the angels explained to Aaron: "When a man is sick, the physician tries to find the cause of the ailment and to remove it. It is easy to light the menorah. Anyone can do that. But it takes a special person to clean the lamps and remove whatever would dim the brightness of the flame. You are like the skillful physician because you will make it possible for the light to burn brightly." Then Aaron was satisfied.

There are two phases to religious life. One is the kindling of the spark of faith. But the more important phase is the cleansing of the heart so that the spark of faith may become a bright flame.

A MITZVAH IS A STEP UPWARD

When you go up to light the lamps . . . (Numbers 8:2).

Rashi interprets *Beha-alotekha* "When you go up to light the lamps," *Shemaa'lah hayta lifne hamenorah* to mean, "There was a step in front of the menorah." The purpose of the step was to uplift the spirit of the Priest when he performed such an important *mitzvah.* Aaron was thus spiritually prepared for his duty.

When a person performs a *mitzvah,* he takes a step up the ladder of religion. Every *mitzvah* should be uplifting. When a boy becomes a *Bar Mitzvah,* he takes his first step, but that must never be his last.

There was a Hasid who liked dancing so well that he danced even during his prayers. When asked why he did this, he answered: "I feel so uplifted and full of enthusiasm, just as if a flame from heaven was kindled within me."

SEE THE GOOD OF JERUSALEM

The manna was like coriander seed . . . (Numbers 11:7).

When anyone came to the late scholar Abraham Kook, Chief Rabbi of Palestine, and gave him discouraging reports about the Holy Land, he would turn away. One day someone asked him: "Why do you turn away from me? These things are true."

"When the Children of Israel were in the desert," Rabbi Kook explained, "they received manna, which our sages called 'bread of the angels.' It was so delicious that anyone eating it thought he was tasting his favorite food. The Children of Israel did not have to expend any effort to procure it and yet many were dissatisfied. Why? Because, according to the Talmud, through this manna the nature of man's character could be detected.

"The righteous man found the manna in his tent. The average man, neither especially righteous or wicked, found the manna a few feet from his tent. But the wicked would have to walk far in order to find it (*Talmud Yoma 75a*). And they were the only ones who spoke disparagingly of the manna. They did not like the manna because it revealed to everyone that they were not righteous.

"Don't be like those who did not like the manna," continued Rabbi Kook. "You see only the defects of the Holy Land. There must also be much good here. That's why I turned away from you. Be like those who enjoyed the manna. Speak of the good! Remember the words of the Psalmist (128:5): 'The Lord bless you out of Zion so that you may see the *good* of Jerusalem all the days of your life.' "

THE PEOPLE'S WELFARE

Send men to scout the land of Canaan . . . of every tribe of their fathers shall you send a man, each one a chieftain (Numbers 13:2).

The *Sidrah Shelah Lekha* tells that Moses sent twelve men to scout the land of Canaan. Ten of them brought back an unfavorable report which disappointed and discouraged the Children of Israel so that they wanted to return to Egypt. These ten failed in their mission because there was fear in their hearts. But in the *Haftarah,* the additional portion read on this Sabbath, we learn that Joshua sent forth two men on a similar mission, and their favorable report succeeded in inspiring the people to conquer Jericho.

Our sages ask: "Why did Moses's mission fail whereas Joshua's succeeded? By virtue of the fact that Joshua was a pupil of Moses, it seems paradoxical that the master's mission should fail whereas the pupil's should succeed. Was Joshua's judgment better than that of Moses?"

The Torah indicates why Moses's mission did not succeed. Joshua selected two men whose names we do not even know. They represented no particular group, whereas Moses selected twelve chieftains. Each chieftain was responsible to his own tribe, and every tribe had a distinct point of view. The twelve chieftains therefore represented twelve different interests, and thus their mission did not succeed.

LOOK FOR THE GOOD

See how the land is that they dwell in, whether it is good or bad . . . (Numbers 13:19).

Ten of the twelve scouts sent by Moses to reconnoiter the land, reported that the prospects were poor. They failed to see the good despite the fact that they brought back a cluster of grapes so large that it had to be carried on a pole over the shoulders of two men.

The Chief Rabbi of the Holy Land invariably welcomed every visitor with the words: "The Lord bless you out of Zion so that you may see the good of Jerusalem all the days of your life" (Psalm 128:5). He then explained that there are some things in the Holy Land that may not seem to be so good, but those who look for the good will find it.

He told the story of a beggar who called on Gershon, a wealthy Jew, and asked him for alms. Gershon asked him where he was from. When the beggar told him he was from Wilna, Gershon exclaimed: "Wilna! I was born in Wilna and I studied there. How are things in Wilna?"

"Very good," replied the beggar. "The Synagogues and schools of learning are flourishing."

Gershon, overjoyed at hearing this, gave the beggar ten rubles. The beggar thanked him and left.

Outside the house, he met another beggar who asked him how the rich man treated him.

"Generously. When he heard I was from Wilna, his native city, he gave me ten rubles."

The second beggar then went in and told Gershon that he was a native of Wilna.

"I, too, come from Wilna," said Gershon. "How are things there?"

"Not so good," replied the beggar. "There are many taverns, gambling houses, cabarets and much immorality."

"Is that so?" remarked Gershon. And he gave the second beggar half-a-ruble. Crest-fallen, the second beggar said: "The other fellow and I are both from Wilna. How is it that you gave him ·ten rubles, and me only half-a-ruble?"

"Ah!" said Gershon. "The other one spoke of Synagogues and schools of learning. Evidently he had been in those places. You tell me about taverns, cabarets and gambling houses; evidently you must have frequented them. So all you deserve is half-a-ruble."

"So," continued the Chief Rabbi, "there is good and bad in every place. Whatever you see depends on your attitude and what you are looking for. Look for the good in people and institutions, and learn to judge every man in the best possible light."

WHY THE THREAD OF BLUE WAS ELIMINATED

Speak to the Children of Israel and instruct them to make for themselves throughout their generations fringes on the corner of their garments, and that they attach a thread of blue to the fringe at each corner (Numbers 15:38).

The fringes which the Children of Israel were to place on each corner of their garments (the *tallit* "prayer shawl"), contained a thread of blue. But for two thousand years the blue thread was omitted because, according to some commentators, the people forgot how to make the blue dye. It seems strange that no one remembered this process since it was an injunction specified in Scriptures. Some say that the blue dye was obtained from a shellfish in Tyre on the Mediterranean, and others maintain that it was extracted from a certain worm. Is it possible that these creatures no longer exist?

The mystics give another reason. They say that the people knew how to make the blue dye, but they did not want to use it because of its association with the rebellion of Korah, of which we read immediately following the injunction concerning the fringes. The conflict between Moses and Korah grew out of his desire to prove that he was a greater scholar than Moses. Korah said to Moses:

"You say that each fringe requires a thread of blue. But suppose a garment is all blue, would the fringes on it still require a thread of blue?" When Moses replied: "Yes, you would still need it," Korah laughed and ridiculed him.

The controversy over the thread of blue, the mystics say, was one of the causes which led to the rebellion of Korah that took the lives of thousands of people, and that is why it was decided not to use the thread of blue because it was associated with this national tragedy.

SEEK PEACE AND PURSUE IT

Moses rose and went to Dathan and Abiram; and the elders of Israel followed him (Numbers 16:25).

Legend recounts that, when Moses asked the elders to accompany him to the tents of Dathan and Abiram, they were amazed that he should be willing to go to them. "They are both trouble-makers," they said, "responsible for the conflict between you and Korah. It is not fitting for you, our leader, to go to these wicked men. Why don't you send a messenger?"

But it was in the spirit of peace that Moses went to Dathan and Abiram. A man of deep humility, who would never allow anything to stand in the way of peace-making, he would not let pride interfere with his goal.

When we reach the conclusion of the *Amidah* prayers and recite the verse: "He who makes peace in the high places, may He make peace for us," it is customary to take three steps backwards. The usual explanation is that, if it is not proper to withdraw from a king or some other high-ranking official by turning our back to him, it is certainly irreverent for us to leave the presence of God by turning our back toward Him.

But there is another explanation: We must never turn our back on peace-making.

Moses was told by God: "Never let pride stand in the way. Peace is paramount."

Mere appeasement is a vain gesture, whereas the conciliatory spirit achieves much. We must *always* "seek peace and pursue it."

A LAND BELONGS TO THOSE WHO MAKE IT LIVE

. . . Behold, the rod of Aaron of the house of Levi had budded, blossomed and borne ripe almonds (Numbers 17:23).

Three clergymen on a visit to the Holy Land asked the Curator of Mount Zion: "Why do the Jews make Jerusalem the capital of the State of Israel? Jerusalem, the cradle of religions and a Holy City belongs to the whole world. It should be an international city. Why do Jews claim it?"

"Let me explain," said the Curator. "The Bible relates that when Moses appointed Aaron as High Priest, the people objected and murmured.

" 'Why should Aaron be selected?' they asked. Whereupon Moses turned to God.

" 'O God, it was You who told me to appoint Aaron. I must now have a miracle to convince the people.'

"God sent an earthquake and Korah and his followers were swallowed up in it. But even then the people refused to accept Aaron's appointment. Then there was a plague but the Children of Israel continued to murmur against Aaron. Finally, God told each tribe to bring a rod and place it in the tent of assembly and Aaron was to place his rod there also. The people were to watch and see which rod would bud and blossom. And when Aaron's rod blossomed, they finally accepted him as High Priest (Numbers 17:16-26).

"Now why did the people accept Aaron when his rod blossomed and bore almonds? Because it showed the vitality of life."

The Curator invited the visiting clergymen to climb up with him to the *Mitzpah*, Mount Zion's Observation Tower. As they looked down, he pointed out:

"From here you can see both the old and the new Jerusalem. In the old, as you can observe, there is desolation: ruins, desert and rocks. On our side is the new Jerusalem where over 150,000 have settled. You can see their new homes, schools, the new hospital and the new university. Everywhere you see life, growth and vitality. You ask to whom does Jerusalem belong. It belongs to those who make it bud and blossom, who make it live and grow.

"The State of Israel is thriving, and the whole land is flourishing because the Israelis are giving it the same loving care that a mother gives her children. This little State, established as recently as 1⌐ ⸴ is now helping other nations which, since then, have acquired ʾeir independence. Israel is today sending to Africa and Asia, physicians, engineers and agricultural experts to help bring life and vitality to these countries so that they, too, may flourish. These specialists, and Israel's ambassadors constitute the first Peace Corps of our time. Ah, yes, my friends, a land belongs to those who make it live."

TO TEACH RATHER THAN TO BEAT

And the Lord spoke to Moses: "Speak to the rock that it give forth water . . . And Moses struck the rock with his rod twice and water came forth abundantly (Numbers 20:7,8,11).

In this *Sidrah* we learn of the grievous error that Moses made when, in order to bring forth water for the thirsty people, he struck the rock instead of speaking to it. But what difference did it make whether he struck the rock or spoke to it? It was vital that he should obtain water. Why then was Moses punished for failing to speak to the rock?

The Lord said to Moses and Aaron: "Because you did not believe in Me to sanctify Me in the eyes of the Children of Israel, therefore you shall not bring this assembly into the land which I have given them" (Numbers 20:12).

What a severe punishment for what appears to be a minor offense!

But there is a deeper meaning behind the incident of Moses's striking the rock, and it points to a significant difference between Judaism and other civilizations.

In order to secure obedience, Pharaoh appointed taskmasters who saw to it that his commands were carried out. This required no education or training. The taskmaster simply said: "Do this, or else." The slaves obeyed as long as the taskmasters were standing over them with whips ready to punish anyone who slackened in his work.

The Children of Israel were given the Torah which recorded for all time the commandments of God and instilled in them Divine instruction. The leaders were to direct the people by speaking to them—not by beating them or employing force as did the Egyptians. The Torah method was to educate people.

The Egyptian method was to force them to do Pharaoh's bidding. When people are stubborn and refuse to do what they should, one way to deal with them is to beat them and the other is to teach them.

Throughout the Bible, we find the expression: "God *spoke* to Moses." In this instance, however, instead of following Divine instruction, our Lawgiver twice struck the rock. Our sages maintain that God said: "My glory lies in teaching, not beating. Because you have used force, you have detracted from My glory and have departed from My method of teaching."

Moses did not carry out this principle and for this reason he was found unworthy to bring the Children of Israel into the Promised Land. Judaism does not countenance the use of force. "Not by might, nor by power, but by My Spirit," says the Lord" (Zechariah 4:6).

MIRACLES REQUIRE HUMAN AID

. . . The Lord sent an angel and brought us forth out of Egypt . . . (Numbers 20:16).

When Theodor Herzl developed his political philosophy of Zionism and urged his people to work for the Jewish State, many pious Jews objected because they believed that only the coming of the Messiah could bring redemption to the persecuted Jews.

Others declared that miracles could not take place unless the people made every effort to help themselves, and they cited the Biblical verse: "We cried unto the Lord who heard our voice, and He sent an angel who brought us out of Egypt" (Numbers 20:16).

Who was this angel? We are told that the angel referred to Moses, the messenger of God. Thus we may derive the understanding that miracles require human help. Just as the miracles in Egypt could not have taken place without Moses the leader, so every generation must have a leader and this leader must be wholeheartedly assisted by the people in accomplishing God's miracles.

THE ASS AND THE ANGEL

And the ass saw the angel of the Lord standing in the way . . . (Numbers 22:23).

The Bible describes the Messiah as a humble man riding on an ass. Why did the Prophet Zechariah (9:9) suggest the lowly ass as the beast that would carry the Messiah? In the story of Balaam (Numbers, Chapter 22), we are told that the ass saw the angel, but that Balaam, the Mesopotamian prophet, did not. While the Bible enumerates a number of animals, only the ass is said to have seen the angel of the Lord. Perhaps it is because, despite the lashing that Balaam inflicted upon the animal, it still carried him on its back.

Sometimes people give the impression of being an ass, an imbecile, or an idiot. Prince Myshkin in Dostoevski's *The Idiot* appears foolish, but is in reality very wise and good. The simple peasant girl in Hauptman's *Der Arme Heinrich* offers her blood to cure her master's leprosy. There are thousands of people who humbly and silently suffer and bend their backs for the good of others. For the merit of such people will the Messiah come.

One who engages in an altruistic cause, or selflessly tries to ease the burdens of others, is often called as ass or an idiot and is ridiculed as a fool. But who knows? It may be that such fools —such asses—may well be the very vehicle that shall carry the long awaited Messiah on their backs.

CONVERTING CURSES INTO BLESSINGS

Baluk (Numbors, Chapters 23 and 24).

According to the interpretation of this *Sidrah*, not only did Balak hate the Jews but Balaam the prophet was also Israel's enemy. If so, why did Moses include the sayings of Balaam in the Torah? Moses was trying to teach us two lessons:

First, that we must learn the value of persistence effectively applied. Balak thrice had to urge Balaam to curse the Israelites before he complied.

Secondly, when God changed the curses into blessings, this was to indicate that the strength of the Jewish people is such that they are able to convert curses into blessings.

When Great Britain withdrew from Palestine, many felt that a curse had been visited upon that country. Bevin, the Labor Prime Minister, was certain that the Arabs would attack and stir up such chaos that the Jews would request the British to return, and this would mean the postponement of the realization of a Jewish Homeland. But instead of a curse, the British departure turned out to be a blessing: the Jews, having defeated all invading armies, at length established the State of Israel.

The test of moral strength is the ability to convert evil into good and, through the teachings of religion, to transform all curses into blessings.

AVOID EXTREMES

Phinehas . . . has turned My wrath away from the Children of Israel . . . (Numbers 25:11).

The story of Phinehas begins in the *Sidrah* of *Balak* (Numbers 22:2-25:9) and ends in the *Sidrah* of *Pinhas* (Numbers 25:10-30:1). What can be the reason for thus interrupting instead of continuing it in one *Sidrah?* The answer is that Phinehas was a zealot and extremist, and not everyone agreed with his methods. The end of the story is therefore reserved for another *Sidrah,* as if to say: "Wait and see. Never hastily accept any extreme position."

In an ordinary Jewish calendar year, the *Sidrot Balak* and *Hukat* are joined. *Mattot* and *Mase* are also joined, but the *Sidrah Pinhas* is never joined with either *Balak* or *Mattot.* This is an intentional illustration of the wisdom of leaving a zealot alone for a while so that no one should hasten to join him. We should always take into account what are the means that the extremist is utilizing to achieve his end, and we must be sure to make certain as to what is his objective.

The Talmud warns against extremism in the following parable: Once an army was marching along a narrow road. On the right was a raging fire and on the left a vast mountain of ice. If the army were to march too close to the right, the flames would consume all of them. If it marched too close to the mountain on the left, the soldiers would all freeze to death. So the soldiers were commanded to march in the exact center of the road; thus they benefited both from the warmth of the fire on the right and from the pleasant coolness of the ice on the left.

THE QUALIFICATIONS OF A LEADER

Let the Lord, Source of the breath of all flesh, appoint over the community someone who will lead them as they go out and as they go in . . . (Numbers 27:16,17).

When a leader was sought for a new youth group organized on Mount Zion, many candidates were considered and all were capable. Some were motivated by extreme points of view; others were aggressive. But Reuben who was finally appointed was of a quiet nature and always perfectly tolerant of others' views. When asked why Reuben was chosen, the Curator replied: "I let myself be guided by the Bible. When Moses asked God to appoint a leader to succeed him, we are told that he said:

" 'Let the Lord, the Source of the breath of all flesh, appoint over the community someone who will lead them as they go out and as they come in; so that the assembly of the Lord shall not be as a sheep without a shepherd' " (Numbers 27:16,17).

The Curator continued: "The Bible uses an unusual expression, *Elohay haruhot l'khol basar* 'the Lord, Source of the breath of all flesh.' Why doesn't it say: 'God, the Creator of the world?' The Bible's exact words are intended to imply that, just as God, the Source of the breath of all flesh, understands every human being, so the leader must not be guided exclusively by his own views. Instead, he must try to understand all the people whom he leads. It is because Reuben possesses such a capacity that we have appointed him to be the leader of the young people's organization."

GOD'S ENEMIES ARE MAN'S ENEMIES

The Lord spoke to Moses, saying: "Take revenge of the Midianites for the Children of Israel; then you shall be gathered to your people." Moses spoke to the people, saying: "Arm your men for war, that they may proceed against Midian, to carry out the Lord's vengeance on Midian" (Numbers 31:1-3).

It will be noted that one verse speaks of the vengeance of Israel, and the other speaks of the vengeance of the Lord. This indicates that the enemies of Israel are the enemies of God, and the enemies of God are the enemies of Israel.

The Midrash emphasizes that the word *Sinai* suggests *sinah* which means the hatred that had been aroused against the Jews because at Mount Sinai they accepted and worshiped the One God (monotheism). This hatred has been expressed over and over again.

Anti-Semites give vent to their hatred by attacking Jews although Judaism is the very source of Christianity. An attack on the Jew is often a prelude to an attack on all religions. The Jew is the first target, and then others are similarly persecuted, as was demonstrated in Nazi Germany. The Nazis began persecuting the Jews and then turned their hatred against Catholics and Protestants alike. Hate begets hate.

ONE PEOPLE WHO SHARE ONE DESTINY

The children of Gad and the children of Reuben said to Moses: "If we have found favor in your sight, let this land be given to your servants as a possession; do not move us across the Jordan." And Moses said to the children of Gad and to the children of Reuben: "Shall your brothers go to war while you stay here?" (Numbers 32:5,6).

This passage is usually interpreted as a rebuke to the tribes of Gad and Reuben. But some authorities feel that Moses was not rebuking them, but was specifically indicating that if some of the Children of Israel were suffering, then the entire people must share their plight. In effect, he was saying: "Do you think it is possible for you to enjoy peace while your brothers are going into battle?"

When the Jews of Persia were threatened with extinction, Mordecai said in like manner to Esther: "Do not think that you will be able to escape in the King's palace more than all the Jews" (Esther 4:13).

Like Moses, Mordecai was obviously saying that the Jews are all one people and regardless of where they live, they all share one destiny.

The Talmud tells us about a Jew who was seen boring a hole under his seat in a boat. When the others in the boat reproved him, he replied: "I am boring a hole under my own seat."

"But," they cried, "this involves us. If the water comes in, all of us will be drowned. We are all in the same boat."

PRIORITY TO THE CHILDREN

The tribes of Gad and Reuben said to Moses: "We shall build sheepfolds here for our cattle, and towns for our little ones, but we ourselves will be armed in the vanguard of the Children of Israel until we have brought them to their place . . ." (Numbers 32:16,17).

When the leader of the two tribes, Gad and Reuben, said: "We shall build sheepfolds here for our cattle, and towns for our little ones," Moses reversed the order and said: "Build towns for your little ones and folds for your sheep . . ." (Verse 24).

Moses thus indicated that priority should always be given to the children—their safety and wellbeing came first. The Jewish people have taken this as their pattern. Whereas it was necessary to provide for all physical needs, the care and education of their children have always been their first consideration.

LOOKING BACKWARD OR FORWARD

These were the wanderings of the Children of Israel who went out of the land of Egypt under the leadership of Moses and Aaron. Moses recorded their departures stage by stage as directed by the Lord; and these are the stages of their departures (Numbers 33:1,2).

Observing that in the first half of the second verse "their departures" is mentioned first, but in the second half "their departures" is mentioned last, one of our sages has interpreted this as indicating two ways of looking at things. One way is to look backward, stressing the place from which we have come; the other is to look forward, constantly keeping in mind our purpose and goal. What was of primary importance was not the journey *from* Egypt, but the journey *to* the Promised Land. Yet the Children of Israel were always remembering Egypt whence they came; they were not particularly concerned about the land to which they were going. Longing for the flesh-pots of Egypt, they again and again murmured against Moses because of the hardships they had to endure in the wilderness. Their minds dwelt far more on what they were missing by leaving Egypt than about the blessings they were to find in the Promised Land. They looked backward and not forward.

About seventy years ago, hundreds of pioneers from eastern Europe settled in Palestine. Looking forward, not backward, these idealists wanted to establish in the land of their ancestors a new life based on the teachings of the Prophets. These pioneers were members of the *Bilu* movement. The name *Bilu* is derived from the first letters of the words in Isaiah: *Bet Ya'akov lekhu venelkha,* "O House of Jacob, let us rise and go . . ." (Isaiah 2:5).

During the Nazi terror in Germany, many Jews went to Palestine merely to escape persecution but, when they arrived there, like the Children of Israel who longed for the flesh-pots of Egypt, many yearned for the comforts they had previously enjoyed.

But, just as the Children of Israel when they approached Mount Sinai began to understand the purpose of their leaving Egypt, today the refugees who have found safety in Israel, fully realize the blessedness of their return to the Holy Land. And they are now exerting all efforts to strengthen the new democratic Jewish State where all may live together in freedom and dignity.

THE FORTY-EIGHT WORDS

The cities which you shall assign to the Levites shall comprise the six cities of refuge which you are to set aside for a manslayer to flee to; and you shall add to these, forty-two more. Thus the total that you assign to the Levites shall be forty-eight cities, with their open land (Numbers 35:6,7).

The purpose of the six cities of refuge was to enable anyone who accidentally killed another, to find refuge and escape the wrath of the victim's kinsmen. The purpose of the forty-two other cities was to provide homes for anyone who wanted to live there a better life.

In our times, there are no such cities of refuge. But the mystics tell us that the forty-eight words in the *Shema* (Deuteronomy 6:4-9) correspond to the forty-eight cities. They say that the *Shema* which emphasizes our love of God and our obligation at all times to carry out the teachings of God, serves the same purpose as the forty-eight cities. When man wants to escape temptation and improve his conduct, he must turn to the *Shema* just as the Israelites could turn to the ancient cities of refuge. The *Shema*, recited twice a day, morning and evening, shall help us day and night to carry out our obligation to obey the commandments of the Lord in both word and deed.

Seated, in the presence of all Israel, Moses places his hands on the shoulder of young Joshua. Having met the test of courage when he was sent to explore Canaan, Joshua has been selected by God to receive the mantle of leadership which for forty years Moses has worn.

Joshua stands in the center in full view of all the men, women, and children in all walks of life, even the hewers of wood and the drawers of water. All are intent upon the words of Moses:

"Go with this people into the land which the Lord has promised to their fathers to give them."

On the horizon above the camp are discernible the features of the whole land of Canaan: the Dead Sea, the Jordan, Lake Tiberias, Haifa, Jaffa, the Mediterranean, and the site of the future city of Jerusalem and the Holy Temple.

The bright shaft suggests the significance and directional purpose of all their wanderings: the religion of the One God.

And Moses called unto . . . . וַיִּקְרָא מֹשֶׁה

Joshua, and said unto him . . . . . . לִיהוֹשֻׁעַ וַיֹּאמֶר

in sight of all Israel: Be . . . . אֵלָיו לְעֵינֵי כָל־

strong and of good courage . . . . יִשְׂרָאֵל חֲזַק וֶאֱמָץ

31:7   לֹא.ד

DEUTERONOMY

When we finish reading the Book of Deuteronomy, we again begin reading Genesis. The significance of this procedure is artistically conveyed by the drawings assigned to Deuteronomy and Genesis: when God's presence permeates our lives, we return to the scene of the ladder in Jacob's dream. Despite all obstacles, we are to ascend from earth to heaven and bring heaven down to earth, and this will result in the ultimate and complete redemption of our people, together with all humanity.

WORDS THAT STING

These are the words which Moses spoke to all Israel . . .
(Deuteronomy 1:1).

The Book of Deuteronomy contains Moses's words of farewell, in which he recalls the murmurings, the waywardness,
and the rebellion of the Children of Israel. To the question:
"Is it proper for a leader to take his farewell by admonishing
and scolding his people?" our sages have answered: "Do not
read *Eleh hadvarim,* 'These are the *words* which Moses spoke,'
but *Eleh hadvorim,* 'These are the *bees.*' Why bees? Because
when a bee stings, it suffers pain and dies."

So it was with Moses. He dearly loved his people and for their
sake gave up his comforts and promising future in the palace
of Pharaoh. For forty years he had led his people and now,
when his end was approaching, he assembled them to hear his
farewell message. He did not want to scold or rebuke them, but
he had to do so because of their backsliding in worshiping the
golden calf and in view of their other moral and religious trans-
gressions. His words were like the stings of bees, and they
brought him great pain. His anguish was so great that, soon
after his farewell address, he died. Like the bees he had given
vent to stinging words and when the sting was delivered, his
life ended.

This is often the lot of leaders who must suffer because there
is need to criticize and reprove, especially when people in general are indifferent and even antagonistic to the spiritual vision
these leaders alone can see.

177

LOVE FREELY GIVEN

DEVARIM (Deuteronomy 1:1-3:22).

This weekly Bible portion, *Devarim* precedes *Tishah B'Av,* which commemorates the destruction of the Temple at Jerusalem.

Rabbi Abraham Kook, former Chief Rabbi of Palestine, loved all Jews, even those who were not observant of their faith.

One day a student who saw Rabbi Kook helping some *halutzim* (pioneers), said to him: "The Bible tells us 'Love your neighbor as yourself' (Leviticus 19:18). I interpret the last word *kamokha* literally—'who is like you,' or 'if he is like you.' If your neighbor is like you—good, pious and scholarly—then you are to love him. But if he is a non-believer, a man who scorns religious practices and the study of the Torah, you are not obligated to love him. Why do you show love to those *halutzim* who are non-observers?"

Rabbi Kook replied: "I can not accept your interpretation that I am to love my neighbor only *when* and *if* he is like me. The true meaning is, 'Love your neighbor *as* yourself.' But if I love someone who is *not* like myself, then my love is *ahavat hinam* 'a love freely given' and without reservation.

"This Sabbath, when we read the *Sidrah Devarim,* is known as *Shabbat Hazon,* the Sabbath of Vision (the first word in Isaiah 1). It precedes *Tishah B'Av,* which commemorates the destruction of the Temple at Jerusalem. Why was the Temple destroyed? It is believed that one of the principal reasons was *sinat hinam* 'causeless hatred.' For that reason, the Temple could not stand and the Jews went into exile.

"Now, the redemption of our people can only be accomplished by the opposite motivation: *ahavat hinam* 'love freely given.' Due to *sinat hinam* we were exiled but with *ahavat hinam,* we pray that we may be worthy of redemption. For this reason we should love the *halutzim* and all people, even though they do not share the same views and do not observe the same religious practices as we do. Only when we finally come to love our neighbor without reservation shall we bring about the redemption of Israel and all mankind."

EVERY PRAYER IS ANSWERED

For what great nation is there that has God so near as is the Lord our God whenever we call upon him? (Deuteronomy 4:7).

When a man goes to his friend's home to ask a favor, his friend is apt to invite him to have tea. The second time he comes, his friend will probably not serve him any tea. The third time, he may let him stand at the door while making his request. And the fourth time, he will probably say to his wife: "Is that man here again? He annoys me." This is the way most human beings react to importunate requests.

But God acts in an entirely different manner. We can come to Him at any time, and He is always ready to hear us. We read in this week's portion: "For what great nation is there that has God so near as is the Lord our God whenever we call upon Him?" The way to God is through prayer. The Psalmist expressed this in the verse: "The Lord is near to them that call upon Him, to all who call upon Him in truth" (145:18).

Every prayer is answered. The story is told of a little girl, Ruth, who saw her doll run over and smashed by a car. Bitterly weeping, she picked up the pieces and carried them home. Her brother, Dan, sympathized with her and said: "That's too bad." As she was going up to her room, he asked: "What are you going to do?"

"I'm going to pray to God to put the pieces together and make my doll whole again," she replied.

"God will not answer your prayer," said Dan.

"Yes, He will," insisted Ruth. About ten minutes later, she came down from her room.

"Well?" asked Dan. "Did God answer your prayer?"

"Yes, He did," she said. "His answer was 'No.'"

In that reply we perceive the essential verity that every prayer is answered. Sometimes God says "Yes"; sometimes "No"; sometimes "Wait a while." God invariably knows what is best for us. Therefore, the man or woman of genuine faith is bound to accept God's answer to his prayer, whatever that answer may be.

LEARNING MUST LEAD TO ACTION

. . . Hear, O Israel, the statutes and the ordinances that I proclaim to you this day, that you may learn them and observe. to do them (Deuteronomy 5:1).

In the above quotation, we observe that learning, or study, is to precede action. The sages of the Talmud discussed the question, "What is more important, study or action?" Rabbi Tarphon said "Action"; Rabbi Akiba said "Study"; because study will lead to action.

A scholar once had a strange dream. He was invited to the palace in heaven. With the key which the angels gave him, he opened the outer gate.

"What a magnificent palace!" he exclaimed, but the palace door was locked. So he knocked and he heard a voice within saying: "You need a key to open this door."

The scholar tried his key, but it did not fit the lock so he again rapped on the door.

"I have the key," he said, "but it does not open this door."

The voice within called out: "That key is for the outer gate only. It is given to those who study but do not practice what precepts they have learned. Knowledge brings you to the outer gate; action brings you into the palace itself."

When he awoke from his dream, he realized the truth of the saying: *Lo hamidrash ikar, ela hamaaseh*—"It is not study but the deed that is primary" (Pirke Avot 1:17).

WHY ARE THE TEN COMMANDMENTS REPEATED?

The Ten Commandments (Deuteronomy 5:6-18).

The Ten Commandments which first appear in Exodus 20 are repeated in *Vaethanan*, the Torah reading of this week. Two explanations for this repetition are given.

One tells us that the first tablets were broken by Moses; therefore, God had to repeat them. Another is based on the interpretation of *p'sal lekha* "carve for yourself" the two tablets (Exodus 34:1). Legend has it that God said to Moses: "Now *you* carve the tablets. You broke the first ones that I had made. Now make your own and they will not be broken."

We are to understand from this that what we make for ourselves we always consider more precious than that which is made for us, and so we carefully guard it.

It is to be noticed that the two versions of the Commandments are not identical. For example, the reason given in Exodus for the observance of the Sabbath is to remind us that God is the Creator of the world. But in Deuteronomy, in this week's *Sidrah*, the reason given is to remind us that we were enslaved in Egypt before God liberated our people.

Another variant is found in the Fifth Commandment. The verse in Deuteronomy is longer. "Honor your father and your mother *as the Lord your God commanded you*, that your days may be long, and *that it may be well with you* upon the land which the Lord your God gives you." The two phrases here italicized do not occur in the version in Exodus.

Why did God command people to honor and love their parents when there is no command for parents to love their children? The mystics believe that all human instincts are derived from Adam. From Adam, they say, we inherit the love of our children, but since Adam had no parents, he could not transmit the love that children should have for their parents. This had to be acquired; therefore, we are commanded to honor and love our parents.

"That it may be well with you," emphasizes the truth that a sound national life must be based upon a wholesome family life. Respect for parents is the foundation of the family and the family is the foundation of society and of the State. Wherever there is respect for parents, there is also respect for authority, and this makes for a strong nation.

DEUTERONOMY 7:12 — 11:25

YOU REALLY GIVE WHEN YOU GIVE OF YOURSELF

*It shall come to pass, because you shall hearken to these or-
dinances and keep and do them, that the Lord your God shall
keep with you the covenant and the mercy which He promised
to your fathers (Deuteronomy 7:12).*

Rashi commented that in the above quotation the word *ekev*
"because," also means "the heel." To hearken and keep God's
ordinances often requires the setting down of the heel (the
foot): such foot service as necessitates physical effort.

When you walk to the Synagogue on the Sabbath, you have
s'khar halikha, the extra *mitzvah* of having exerted physical
effort. To make the pilgrimage to Jerusalem three times a year
was considered a great *mitzvah* because people had to go there
al regel "by foot." Those going to Jerusalem fulfilled this *mitzvah* by walking, the exercise of an extra effort in making the
pilgrimage.

The term for the privilege of being called to the Torah is
aliyah, which means "going up." Returning to Zion is also
aliyah "going up." There is the well known Youth Aliyah Movement. And those who return to Zion are called *olim* because
they "go up" to the Land.

Mitzvot shehadam dash ba'akevov—"There are *mitzvot* which
man carries out by using his feet": that is, by extra physical
effort.

Likewise, there are several ways of helping others. One is to
send a check to the Federation of Charities. Another is to go
with a man in need, and help him get a job. Still another is
to go to the man's home and take a personal interest in him.
That *mitzvah* is greatest in which a man gives of himself.

Kahlil Gibran said: "You give but little when you give of
your possessions. It is only when you give of yourself that you
really give."

GOD IS THE GREAT HEALER

The Lord will remove all sickness from you . . . (Deuteronomy 7:15).

A sad and disheartened member of a Hasidic congregation came to his Rabbi with his sorrow.

"My child is very sick and the doctor has given up hope. What shall I do?"

The Rabbi replied:

"God gives the doctor the mission to heal. God never gives the doctor permission to give up hope. The physician is only God's agent for healing. *The great Healer is God.*"

What is claimed to be incurable today may well be curable in the near future.

A sick woman said to her friend: "I don't know what to do. I pray to God every day but He doesn't seem to hear my prayer."

Her friend encouraged her with these words: "He heard you. Just be patient. God has so many things to do. Just wait until He gets around to you."

RIGHTEOUSNESS IS ITS OWN BLESSING

Beware lest you forget the Lord your God . . . (Deuteronomy 8:11).

The Bible frequently warns man not to permit the wealth he has acquired to make him arrogant, and repeatedly charges him never to forget his debt of gratitude to God.

Thus are we admonished in this *Sidrah Ekev:*

"You shall eat and be satisfied and thank the Lord your God for the good land which He has given you. Beware lest you forget the Lord your God and fail to keep His commandments, His ordinances and His statutes which I enjoin upon you this day; lest when you have eaten and are satisfied, and have built fine houses to live in, and your herds and flocks have multiplied, and your silver and gold have increased and everything you own has prospered, then beware lest your heart become haughty and you forget the Lord your God . . . and you say in your heart: 'My own power and the might of my own hand have brought me this wealth.' Remember that it is the Lord your God who gives you the power to get wealth . . ." (Deuteronomy 8:10-14, 17,18).

A Hasid came to his Rabbi for a blessing. The Rabbi prayed that God grant the Hasid a life of kindness and righteousness and the joy of fulfilling the *mitzvot.*

"What about blessing me with wealth?" asked the Hasid.

"Wealth is not always a blessing," replied the Rabbi. "Much depends upon how we use our wealth. It may be a blessing or it may be a curse. Only the good life based on the *mitzvot* is a blessing. Thus when I pray that God grant you a life of kindness and righteousness and the joy of fulfilling the *mitzvot,* I give you the greatest blessing of all."

Wealth often makes people selfish and arrogant. When Bernard Baruch made his first million, he was proud of his achievement, but his father was not at all impressed and asked: "My son, what are you going to do with this wealth? It is a material achievement to accumulate wealth, but it is a spiritual achievement to put it to good and unselfish use."

SERVE GOD WITH YOUR WHOLE HEART

. . . Love the Lord your God and serve Him with all your heart and with all your soul (Deuteronomy 11:13).

Why is the word *l'vavkha* "your heart" in the expanded form and not in the simple form *lib'kha?* Because man is born with two inclinations, one for doing good and one for doing evil, and we are to serve God *bishnay yitzrekha b'yetzer tov ub'yetzer hara* with both inclinations, the good and the evil" (*Talmud Berakhot*).

The son of the Rabbi of Chortkoff was a bright child, but a few days before he was to become a Bar Mitzvah, he was sad.

"Why are you so sad?" asked his father. "You know that an important guest is now coming into your life, the *yetzer tov* 'the good impulse.' "

"But," said his son, "the *yetzer tov* has a partner, *yetzer hara* 'the evil impulse.' As long as the good partner was not present, the evil partner had no reason to enter my life. But now that the good partner is coming, the evil partner will also come."

His father explained: "Very often in life, my son, you will be tempted to do wrong. That's your evil impulse. You must cultivate the will power to overcome this evil impulse so that the good may prevail. That is why in the command, 'to love God and serve Him with all your heart,' the word for *your heart* is not in the singular but in the plural, not *lib'kha* but *l'vavkha*. This indicates that we are to love and serve God with both impulses.

"Inclinations are not evil per se. It all depends on what use we make of them. Let me give you an illustration:

"A horseman has three alternatives in the treatment of his wild horses. He may let them loose where they will cause harm and damage; he may lock them up in his stable; or he may train and harness them to do his work. So it is with our instincts and inclinations. Setting them loose is license; locking them up is repression; putting them to good use is discipline—the sole way to live a good and righteous life."

WE STUDY THE TORAH
WHEN WE LIVE BY ITS PRECEPTS

You shall teach your children the words of God, speaking of them when you stay at home and when you are away, when you lie down and when you rise up (Deuteronomy 11:19).

A merchant once said to the Kotzker Rabbi: "I am extremely busy every day earning a living for my wife and children. But according to this verse, I must study Torah all day long. How can I do it?"

The Kotzker Rabbi replied: "The verse does not mean that you are to neglect your business. When you fulfill the principles of the Torah in your everyday activities, when you are honest in all your dealings, in your weights and measures, when your word is your bond, and you promptly pay your employees' wages —then it is considered as though you were studying Torah.

"Remember that in the future world, the first question asked of us is not, 'Were you a firm believer?' or 'What observances did you practice?' but 'Were you honest in your dealings with your fellow men?' If the spirit of God prevails in all your deeds, you are practicing the teachings of the Torah. God is not only in the Synagogue. He is also in the home, in the market place, in courts of justice, and in all our relationships with our fellow men. God is with us either everywhere or nowhere!"

WHAT I DO AFFECTS ALL MANKIND

See, I set before you this day, blessing and curse (Deuteronomy 11:26).

"You hold the key to the world," said a Rabbi addressing a Bar Mitzvah. "Upon you the future of mankind depends. We read in this week's *Sidrah:* 'See, I set before you this day, blessing and curse.' It is interesting to note that the verse in Hebrew begins with *Re-ay* 'See' which is in the singular, and continues with the word *lifnekhem* 'you' which is in the plural. We may take this to indicate that the wellbeing of the entire community depends upon every individual. One man can exert upon his fellow men a tremendous influence for good or for evil. The course of history has been changed both by Pharaoh and Moses, by Haman and by Mordecai, by Hitler and by Churchill. Wars have often been started and ended by a single individual."

When mankind is judged, we shall learn that the deeds of one man can affect the fate of all mankind. *Asah mitzvah ahat ashray sheh-hikhria et atzmo v'khol haolam l'khaf z'khut* "He who does one good deed may tip the scale on the side of merit for himself and for all mankind" (*Kedushin 40*b).

The Talmud also tells us that a man should always say: *Bishvili nivra haolam* "The world was created for my sake."

If everyone were to feel that his own deeds could determine the fate of mankind, he would live with a sense of greater responsibility for his least act, and the world would be a far better place in which to live.

GOD REPAYS US TENFOLD
FOR THE TITHE WE GIVE

*You shall surely set aside every year a tenth part of all the
yield of your produce (Deuteronomy 14:22).*

Commenting on the injunction that every Israelite is to give
away one-tenth of his yearly produce (see also Numbers 18:26-
30), our sages say that God invariably repays the giver tenfold.

The Hofetz Hayim tells the story of the peasant who came
to the city to sell his stock of seed. On the scale the merchant
placed as a weight, a shekel to balance the amount of seed.
For every shekel the merchant placed on the scale, he was to
pay the peasant ten shekels. But when the merchant glanced
aside, the ignorant peasant pocketed three coins from the scale.
The three coins had some value, but the peasant did not realize
that the merchant would now pay him thirty coins less for his
seed. The peasant was stealing from himself.

"Likewise," said the Hofetz Hayim, "the Jew who does not
give his tithe is like the peasant who thinks he has enriched
himself with a few coins, but has actually deprived himself of
much more, because in some way, God repays us tenfold for
all the charity we do."

In like fashion, the Kotzker Rabbi interpreted the commandment, "You shall not steal," to mean not only "Do not steal
from others," but also "Do not steal from yourself." He who
does not contribute his fair share to charity is stealing from himself.

REJOICE IN YOUR FESTIVAL

You shall rejoice in your festival . . . (Deuteronomy 16:14).

With reference to the Festival of Sukkot, the Bible says: *V'samahta b'hagekha* "You shall rejoice in your festival." And in the following verse we are told: "You shall be altogether joyful." Both Passover and Shavuot are equally important and happy festivals, yet in this same weekly portion there is no mention of rejoicing on Passover (16:1-8). And with regard to Shavuot, we are told only once "You shall rejoice before the Lord your God" (16:11). Therefore we wonder why Sukkot is singled out for special reference in two verses. Since Sukkot is also called *Hag Heh-asif,* the Feast of Ingathering, or the Harvest Festival, the command "to rejoice" seems superfluous. When the crops are harvested, it is only natural that we should rejoice.

Obviously, there must be a reason why the Bible so specifically bids us to rejoice on Sukkot.

A city Rabbi, wanting to see the peasants at their joyful harvest festivities, spent the day in a small village and while there, talked to a peasant whom he saw gazing at the ingathering of his own rich harvest. To his amazement, he found that the peasant seemed perturbed.

"What's the matter?" asked the Rabbi.

"I thought my crop was going to be much larger," said the peasant, "and I'm terribly disappointed."

In the course of his rounds, the Rabbi came upon another peasant who was also unhappy.

"Why are you downcast?" he asked.

"Just look at my harvest!" the peasant replied. "My neighbor's is twice as large."

Then the Rabbi understood why the Bible twice commands: "You shall rejoice." The first injunction is directed to greedy people like the first peasant and the second injunction, to those who, like the other peasant, are envious.

It is significant that the Hebrew word *V'samahta* "You shall rejoice," though addressed to all the people, is not expressed in the plural but in the singular. This implies that a man shall find joy within himself and in his own harvest and, without greed or envy, rejoice in his neighbor's good fortune. We should remember the admonition in *The Ethics of the Fathers:* "Who is rich? *Hasameah b'helko* He who rejoices in his own portion."

Only if a man is neither envious nor greedy can he truly rejoice.

GOD OUR SUPREME COMMANDER

When you go forth to battle . . . (Deuteronomy 20:1-8).

It is said that the students of a famous Yeshiva once ridiculed the draft laws that are cited in the *Sidrah Shofetim*.

Four categories of men were exempt from serving in the army: those who had just built a home; those who had just planted a vineyard; those who had recently married; and those who were faint-hearted. The students laughed at this.

"What kind of an army would remain after all these exemptions?" they asked. "Suppose the quota were 100,000. About ten per cent of the young people must recently have built new homes, and that would exempt 10,000. It is easy enough to plant a vineyard, and this would eliminate about 20,000 more. Most people marry at an early age, and these exemptions would amount to about 40,000. And who is not afraid and faint-hearted when it comes to war? That would exclude at least 15,000 more.

"The Talmud says that exemptions were allowed not only for those who were faint-hearted because of the dangers of war, but also for those who feared to go into battle because of the sins they had committed. Then who would be left? None but the commander-in-chief with three or four soldiers who, like the Wilner Gaon, the Baal Shem Tov, Hazon Ish, and the Hofetz Hayim, were without sin."

When Reb Hayim Brisker heard these cynical remarks, he reproved them:

"This is not a jest. If we had an army of saints and scholars such as the Baal Shem Tov, Hofetz Hayim, Hazon Ish and the Wilner Gaon, we could conquer the strongest army in the world." Another Rabbi, overhearing this, added his opinion:

193

"Even these saints and scholars would not remain in the army because, in view of their humility and modesty, they would not claim that they had never committed a sin. The commander-in-chief alone would be left to fight. But with God as our supreme Commander, we would still be victorious.

"The strength of the Jew is not in numbers. The strength of the Jew is his faith and trust in God."

BELIEF AND ACTION MUST BE CONSISTENT

When you go forth to battle . . . (Deuteronomy 20:1-8).

Commenting on those exempt from serving in the army, the Talmud adds another category: *Hasah ben t'fillah lit'fillah averah hi b'yado, v'hozer aleha m'orkhay hamilhamah*—"He who talks between the placing of the *tefillin* (phylacteries) on the hand and on the head cannot serve in the army" (*Sota 44*b).

Whether that injunction was literally carried out or not, symbolically it conveys a profound thought. The *tefillin* on the hand suggests action. The *tefillin* on the head represents thought or belief. There must be no interruption, no dichotomy, no division between our belief and our action. There must be no inconsistency: our actions must never belie our beliefs, but be based directly upon them. We must not think one way and act another.

When we place the *tefillin* on the hand, we are reminded that our deeds should be holy. When we place the *tefillin* on the head, we are to remember that our thoughts should be holy. Thought and action should always be uniform.

BLESSED IS HE WHO HAS WORTHY HEIRS

It shall come to pass on that day that a man bequeaths to his sons that which he possesses . . . (Deuteronomy 21:16).

This verse begins with the word *v'haya* "It shall come to pass." Our Rabbis tell us that any verse which begins with the word *v'haya* refers to a joyous occasion. Yet this verse speaks of death and inheritance. Is that a happy occasion? Man can truly rejoice if he knows that when he departs this life, he will leave behind worthy heirs who will use their inheritance to perpetuate the ideals and purposes to which he dedicated his life.

Happy indeed is the man who knows that he leaves behind heirs worthy of his love, trust and sacrifices.

THE REBELLIOUS CHILD

If a man has a stubborn and rebellious son who will not heed the voice of his father or the voice of his mother and does not obey them even after they discipline him . . . (Deuteronomy 21:18).

Our sages comment that the voice of both father and mother must be in unison, thus implying that both must live and act in harmony. If this is so, and the son is rebellious, then the son is at fault. If, however, there is discord in the home and the parents constantly bicker and quarrel, then the rebellious son is not to be blamed. It is the parents who are at fault. They are to be held responsible for the behavior of their child. We hear so much nowadays about juvenile delinquency. We must realize there is also adult delinquency. The parents' good example is necessary. "Character is not taught; it is caught."

CONVERT CURSES INTO BLESSINGS

These shall stand upon Mount Gerizim for the blessing of the people . . . And these shall stand upon Mount Ebal for the curse . . . (Deuteronomy 27:12,13).

Later, in verses 13 to 26 of Chapter 27, the Bible records in detail the "curse" known as the *to-khe-hah* "the rebuke."

When people were superstitious and declined the honor of being called to the Torah for this portion, the *aliyah* was usually given to the *shamash* (sexton). One *shamash* complained:

"If there is a rebuke and a curse, who is to blame? Is it not the Rabbi who should have taught the people to live righteously? The Rabbi should be given this *aliyah*."

He was told that Rabbi Levi Yitzhak of Berditchev once took this *aliyah,* not because he felt that the Rabbi is to blame if the people sin, but because the Rabbi's task is to convert curses into blessings. His action was based on verse 27:8 that the Children of Israel shall inscribe upon the stones all the words of this law *ba-er hetev* "with a good explanation." And he interpreted *ba-er hetev* to mean "an explanation that will bring good." In other words, that we should extract the good from the evil.

There is a legend that whenever King David repented his sins, each tear that he shed became a pearl. There were 150 pearls corresponding to the 150 Psalms. David thus converted the evil of his sins into everlasting good.

Likewise, a great leader can convert curses into blessings. For this reason Rabbi Levi Yitzhak of Berditchev accepted this *aliyah*. A precedent was established, and in some congregations the Rabbi takes this *aliyah* in the hope that he may succeed in guiding his people so that evil may be converted into good.

THE BLESSINGS THAT PURSUE US

*All these blessings shall come upon you and overtake you
if you will but heed the word of the Lord your God (Deuteronomy 28:2).*

On one occasion, a student said to his Rabbi: "This verse,
that blessings shall overtake you, puzzles me. It indicates that
men run away from blessings. We hear of men running away
from curses. But whoever runs away from a blessing? The same
question arises in Psalm 23: 'Surely, goodness and mercy shall
pursue me all the days of my life.' I just don't understand why
one would run away from these blessings."

To this the Rabbi replied: "When the Nazis were about to
capture Poland, many Jews refused to leave that country. They
were reluctant to leave behind their possessions, become penniless, and be compelled to start life anew in a strange land. They
would be confronted by countless dangers involved in crossing
borders, and they would have to wander through many countries
before they could get to Palestine.

"Every day one of my friends used to urge me: 'Come, let us
go to Palestine today!' I kept postponing our journey, but he
was persistent, and finally, together with him, I left Poland.
His urging was indeed a blessing that pursued me. Had he gone
without me, I might well have remained until the Nazis entered Warsaw and drove all the Jews into the Ghetto, and I
would have perished.

"How true it is that blessings sometimes run after us! We
often procrastinate before taking constructive action to carry
out our best ideas. We are not sure that a certain idea is good,
so we seem to be running away from it. We should therefore
pray that our ideas may be blessings, and that they will pursue
us and finally overtake us."

TO STAND STILL IS TO REGRESS

You stand this day all of you before the Lord your God . . .
(Deuteronomy 29:9).

One portion of the *Sidrah Nitzavim* (Deuteronomy 29:18-28)
contains the *to-khe-hah* "the rebuke," as does the previous
Sidrah Kee Tavo (Deuteronomy 27:15-26; 28:15-69). But the
passage beginning the *Sidrah Nitzavim* seems to interrupt these
rebukes: "You stand this day all of you before the Lord your
God: the heads of your tribes, your elders, and your officials,
even all the men of Israel" (29:9). But this verse is actually
also a rebuke because standing still is retrogression. If we are
not making progress in our studies, in the pursuit of our ideal,
in our institutional and civic work, we are regressing. To stand
in the same place all the time is deserving of a rebuke.

Concerning the study of Torah, Rabbi Shimon ben Lakish
found these words in a hidden scroll: *Im taazveni yom, yo-
mayim a-ezvekha* "If you neglect me one day I will neglect you
two days" (*Yerushalmi Brakhot*).

200

WE ARE ALL EQUAL BEFORE GOD

You stand this day all of you before the Lord your God . . .
(Deuteronomy 29:9).

When the Nazis were searching for the Rabbi of Belz, to
place him in a concentration camp, one of his disciples, determined to save him, put on the Rabbi's clothes and pretended
that he was the Rabbi of Belz. The Nazis consigned him to a
concentration camp, but when the Rabbi heard of this, he was
greatly distressed and collected funds with which to ransom his
disciple. When the liberated disciple came to see him, the Rabbi
asked: "Why did you risk your life for me?"

"You are a renowned Rabbi," replied the disciple, "and our
most esteemed leader. I wanted to save you because you are far
more important and more greatly needed than I am."

"I appreciate your loyalty," said the Rabbi, "but when it
comes to *Kiddush Hashem* 'sanctifying God's name,' especially
if it involves suffering or death, one is no more important than
another. The Bible tells us: 'You stand all of you before the
Lord your God: the heads of your tribes, your elders, and your
officials, even all the men of Israel' (Deuteronomy 29:10). Our
religion teaches us that before God, when His name is to be
sanctified, no one is superior or inferior; all of us are equal."

STANDING BEFORE GOD

You stand this day all of you before the Lord your God: the heads of your tribes, your elders and your officials, even all the men of Israel (Deuteronomy 29:9), your children, your wives, even the stranger within your camp, from the hewer of your wood to the drawer of your water (Deuteronomy 29:10).

Why does the Bible divide the above passage into two verses? Logically the two verses should be combined into one verse, but by dividing them, a new idea is stressed. Not only when every man, but when every child, every woman and even the stranger are treated with dignity and respect, *then* we stand before the Lord our God.

When we make distinctions and discriminate against people because of race or color or origin, and when we deny them human rights, we do *not* stand before the Lord our God. The same applies to all who occupy positions of responsibility. When they regard all human beings as created in the image of God and entitled to the same rights and privileges they ask for themselves, they are truly standing before God.

WRONGDOING IN THE NAME OF GOD

For I know how defiant and stiffnecked you are; even now while I am still alive with you in your midst, you have been defiant against the Lord . . . (Deuteronomy 31:27).

The Hebrew phrase *im Adonai* is translated, "against the Lord." Literally, it means "with the Lord."

How often do people commit sins in the name of the Lord!

Rashi, quoting *Tanhumah* on Genesis 37:33, tells us that when his ten brothers sold Joseph as a slave, they vowed to ostracize anyone who might tell their father or others what they had done. As they were about to take that vow, Reuben walked away, and only nine were left. A *minyan* (quorum of ten) was needed before they could make that vow; therefore, they included God in the *minyan*. They did evil not only "against God," but "with God."

History is replete with horrible incidents in which, in the name of religion, crimes were committed: so-called witches were hanged, those of another faith were massacred and thousands were burned at the stake.

There have been two stages in the development of human relations: "Live and destroy," and "Live and let live." We are now entering the third stage: *"Live and help live."*

GROUNDLESS FEARS

*For I know that after my death, you will act wickedly and
turn aside from the way which I have commanded you, and
that in time to come, misfortune will befall you for having
done evil in the sight of the Lord and vexed Him by your deeds
(Deuteronomy 31:29).*

Moses feared that the succeeding generation, under Joshua,
would be worse than that of his own day. It seemed to be a
logical assumption. If this generation that had had Moses as a
teacher and had received at his hands the Ten Commandments,
had nevertheless committed evil, how much more likely that
the next generation, deprived of Moses, would be far more
sinful.

Despite Moses's apprehension, the succeeding generation,
under the leadership of Joshua, turned out to be a good generation.

"Israel served the Lord all the days of Joshua, and all the
days of the elders that outlived Joshua, and had known all that
the Lord had done for Israel" (Joshua 24:31).

Why was this so? When a person is attacked, he defends himself. When he is told that he cannot do a certain thing, it frequently becomes a challenge, and he says: "I will show you."
This was true of the generation after Moses. When the people
were told that they would be wicked, they resolved to be righteous.

We are often told that the present generation is indifferent
to the religious ideals of morality and ethical standards; that it
is primarily concerned with pleasure and frivolity; and that the
next generation will be worse. But it may well be that the
next generation will follow the example of Joshua's generation
and prove that it can be the best generation in American Jewish history.

In Israel some leaders are saying that, because many of the
present generation are disinterested in religious observance, the

next generation will be worse. But there are many indications
that the next generation, as did the generation under Joshua,
will accept these accusations as a challenge and, contrary to all
predictions, turn out to be one of the best in all Jewish history.

THE WATCHMAN OF THE WORLD

You neglected the Rock that begot you,
And forgot the God who created you (Deuteronomy 32:18).

Rabbi Bunim tells the story of a King who had an exceptionally beautiful garden and commissioned a famous artist to paint a picture of it for future generations to admire. The artist portrayed every detail: the trees, flowers, fountains, even the apples on the trees and the watchman in the garden. The picture looked precisely like a living garden.

The King was so pleased with the painting that he invited the artist to view it when it was hung on a wall in the palace. While they were admiring the painting, some birds flew in through the open window and began pecking at the apples on the canvas.

"How wonderful!" exclaimed the King. "Even the birds think it is real!"

The artist, however, was keenly disappointed and said: "The picture is not real because the birds do not see the watchman who is there to guard the tree."

Rabbi Bunim continued: "Alas, most of us are like the birds! Because God is not real to us, we never see the Watchman of the world. We all see the beautiful things that have been placed in our world, but frequently we are unaware of God who created them all."

SO FEW ARE SEEKING GOD

God said: "I will hide My face from them . . ." (Deuter-onomy 32:20).

The Rabbi of Meseritz once saw a child weeping under a tree in a garden.

"Why are you crying?" he inquired.

"Nobody's looking for me!" replied the child.

The Rabbi was puzzled. "What do you mean?" he asked.

"My friends and I are playing 'Hide and Seek.' I am hiding, but nobody's looking for me. They must have all gone away."

The Rabbi reflected: "I heard in this child's voice, the voice of the *Shekhinah* God's Spirit: 'Nobody's looking for Me.'

OUR ACTS MAY DETERMINE OUR DESTINY

God said: "I will hide my face from them;
I will see what their end will be . . ." (Deuteronomy 32:20).

Rabbi Pinkas commented on this verse as follows: "Everyone thinks about his end, and God acts in accordance with everyone's thoughts concerning the day of his death.

"Zebulun gave so much money to charity that his wife complained to me. 'When Zebulun is old,' she said, 'what will happen? We may have to depend on charity ourselves.'

"When I asked her husband: 'Why are you giving so much to charity?' Zebulun replied: 'I have no way of telling when my end will come. Who knows? Perhaps it may be tomorrow! Therefore I want to give to charity today.'

"In the same city lived Shmaryahu, a miser. When called upon to give charity, he said: 'I have no way of telling when my end will be, and I do not want to be destitute twenty years hence; therefore I cannot give charity now.'

"From this I concluded that in heaven the angels protect everyone from his fears. Zebulun, who was afraid that he might soon die and so gave charity every day that he lived, was granted a long life. Shmaryahu, who thought that he might live long, and therefore did not give charity for fear he would not have enough for his old age, was decreed a short life.

"The verse, 'I will see what their end will be' means that God always looks to see how one's thoughts about his end are influencing his life, and He deals with man accordingly. Our acts may determine our destiny."

PERSECUTION WILL CEASE

I will heap evils upon them;
I will use up My arrows upon them (Deuteronomy 32:23).

When the Children of Israel heard this prediction, they were frightened and cried out: "How shall we be able to endure so much? How can we face such suffering?"

There is a legend that, in order to console them, Moses brought them to the arsenal of God and showed them all kinds of weapons, so numerous that they could not be counted. He explained that of all these weapons only the arrows were limited in number. The meaning of the verse *Hitzai akhaleh bam* "I will use up My arrows upon you" is *Hitzai khalim v'hem enam kalim* "My arrows will be used up, but they (the Children of Israel) shall remain."

The Jew has a profound faith that all his sufferings will come to an end and, despite every affliction he has endured throughout the ages, that day will come when all the arrows of adversity shall be spent and persecution will cease.

EVERY COMMUNITY IS IMPORTANT FOR TORAH

The Lord came down from Sinai,
And rose from Seir unto them;
He shone forth from Mount Paran . . . (Deuteronomy 33:2).

A famous Rabbi went everywhere, even into the smallest communities in order to teach Torah. One of his disciples asked:

"Is it fitting that you, a famous Rabbi, should be concerned with such small Synagogues? Should you not give your time and efforts to the big cities where you can reach many more people?"

"I have a precedent for what I am doing," replied the Rabbi. "In the Bible we read: 'The Lord came down from Sinai and rose from Seir unto them; He shone forth from Mount Paran.' So you see, God's Presence was not only on Mount Sinai but also journeyed from Sinai to Seir, the hill country of Edom, then through Paran, the mountain range south of Canaan, and even through the desert, until the *Shekhinah* reached the Promised Land. Man can do nothing better than try to emulate God. Every community is a vital link in the chain of Judaism. We must provide spiritual sustenance to every town, village and hamlet, however small.

THE TASK OF THE TRUE LEADER

The Lord said to Moses: "This is the land which I promised Abraham, Isaac, and Jacob, saying: I will give it to your off-spring. I have let you see it with your own eyes, but you shall not go over there" (Deuteronomy 34:4).

It is usually explained that Moses was not allowed to enter the Promised Land because he had sinned by striking the rock instead of speaking to it, to make it give forth water (Numbers 20:7,12).

Another explanation is that Moses could not enter the Promised Land because he spoke ill of his people and called them "rebels" (Numbers 20:10).

Isaiah also was punished for speaking ill of his people. Our sages say that when Isaiah said: "I dwell among a people of unclean lips" (6:5), his tongue was touched with a glowing stone because he had uttered these harsh words against his people.

Similarly, say the sages that Elijah spoke ill of his people and was punished. When he said: "I alone am left faithful to the Lord," he was commanded by God: "Go to Damascus and anoint Elisha as a Prophet in your stead" (1 Kings 19:14-17).

The leader of his people must criticise them with love. To call the people "rebels," or men of "unclean lips," is to show scorn and contempt, and such taunts never bring out the good in others but always increase their anger and rebellion.

The task of the true spiritual leader is to administer chastisement with compassion and trust. Even while he criticises his followers, he must always let them feel that he has faith in them.

CLOSING NOTE

I will give thanks to the Lord with all my heart (Psalm 111:1).

The Masoretic note at the conclusion of the Five Books of Moses tells us that one word will help us remember that the Book of Deuteronomy contains thirty-four chapters. That word *levav* "heart" which has the numerical value of thirty-four, occurs in the verse: "I will give thanks to the Lord with all my heart." What an appropriate thought for the conclusion of the Five Books of Moses! When we complete the Reading of the Torah, our hearts are suffused with the spirit of God. We praise God and thank Him, the Source of all life, reality and righteousness.

The Hebrew word for "heart" is not in the singular but in the plural, not *lev* but *levav*. This is to indicate that man's heart has two impulses: *yetzer tov* "the good impulse" and *yetzer hara* "the evil impulse." When he studies Torah and carries out its teachings, his heart, though it may be inclined to evil, becomes good and he thanks God with both impulses.

Before studying Torah, man may not be inclined to change his evil impulse but, after studying Torah, the evil impulse becomes good and his whole heart acknowledges God and follows His precepts.

"I have bad inclinations. How can I break them?" said Reuben to his Rabbi. And the Rabbi replied:

"Do not try to break your inclinations. They may break you before you can ever succeed in breaking them. Guide and direct your inclinations and use them for good purposes. The purpose of the Torah is to help man to transform his evil impulses into good ones. *Lo nitnu hamitzvot ela letzaref bohen et habriyot* "The mitzvot were given for the sole purpose of improving man's character" (*Bereshit Rabba 44*).

It is also well to remember that the last letter of the *Sidrah V'zot Habrakhah*, the last portion of the Five Books of Moses, is *lamed* and the first letter which begins the Five Books, is *bet*. *Lamed* and *bet* spell the word *lev* "heart." This is to impress upon us that God has promised man: "I shall remove your heart of stone, and I will give you a heart of flesh" (Ezekiel 36:26).

The Torah is God's remedy for man's spiritual illness. It can transform the heart of stone into a heart of flesh and compassion. It can break down human callousness and make man what he should be.

When we complete reading the Torah and begin to re-read it, we say: "I will give thanks to the Lord with all my heart." In this way we acknowledge that we understand its message and shall take the teachings of the Torah to our heart to inspire and guide us.

חגים ומועדים

HOLIDAYS

NOTE ON THE ORNAMENTAL TITLES FOR THE HOLIDAYS

The Holy Land is known for the pomegranate, remarkable for its beautiful colors, lovely blossoms and comely fruit.

The various seasons bring about fascinating changes in nature. The artist uses the motif of the pomegranate in the titles for the Holy Days and Festivals from Selihot until Shavuot, in order to suggest the seasonal changes and the succession of the Holidays in the Land of Israel.

THE TALLIT OF GOD

A few hours before the midnight *Selihot* Service on Saturday night preceding Rosh Hashanah, a group of devout Jews who had recently come to Israel from European concentration camps, felt the urge to hold the *Selihot* Service in the Synagogue on Mount Zion. Because Mount Zion is close to the Jordan border, it was not safe for anyone to assemble there after nightfall. But they were determined to hold this Service in the Synagogue near King David's tomb close by the Chamber of Destruction in which the ashes of innocent Jews, massacred by the Nazis, are preserved in large urns.

In the dark, the worshipers found the Synagogue but to their dismay, they had forgotten to bring a *tallit* (prayer shawl) and to invite a *Hazan* (Cantor) to officiate.

Reuben, who had organized the Service said: "I have heard that on Mount Zion King David himself will be the *Hazan* if no other *Hazan* is available. All we need is a good *Baal Tefillah*, a pious Jew who is familiar with the Service and able to chant."

"Baruch is a pious Jew," someone mentioned. "He officiated in our camp and we were heartened and inspired." Baruch was thus appointed to be the *Baal Tefillah*.

"What shall we do about a *tallit?*" Baruch asked.

Hayim, who came from Bergen-Belsen called out: "I heard the Kotzker Rabbi say that when there is no *tallit*, take the *Tallit* of God."

"The *Tallit* of God!" Baruch exclaimed. "How can you take the *Tallit* of God? Where is it to be found?"

"I have it right here," said Hayim. "In camp, even in winter we were given no bedding or blankets, but some one persuaded the Nazi captain to allow us a sheet for a sick man. When he recovered, the sheet was given to others who were sick. Miraculously, the sick always recovered. When several were sick on the same night, the sheet was given to one sick person for a few hours, and then to another, and so on. All the sick recovered. In all those four years at camp, the sheet was always clean and never torn. Everyone called it 'The *Tallit* of God.' I have brought it with me."

In the dark, he unwrapped the package he carried, and the sheet shone like a beam of moonlight. Hayim handed it to Baruch, and a hush fell over the gathering as Baruch recited the blessing over the *tallit* and began to chant. Never before had they heard such a stirring and inspiring *Selihot* Service.

"No wonder!" said Reuben. "It was King David's voice we heard. He was the *Hazan,* and the *tallit* was that of *Mara d'alma* 'the Master of the world.' "

AWAKE, YOU SLEEPERS!

In many Synagogues, especially in Eastern Europe, the *Selihot* Service was held not at midnight but in the early hours of the morning while it was still dark, and ended at sunrise. People had no alarm clocks to arouse them and had to depend on the *shamash* (sexton) of the Synagogue, who would go from house to house, knock on all doors, and announce it was time for the *Selihot* Service. The Chief Rabbi of Warsaw once called together all the *shamashim* and instructed them to knock on every door until the door was opened, but one of them said:

"We usually knock on the door, announce the Service and then go on to the next house. We never wait until the door is opened. Is that necessary?"

Thereupon the Rabbi told him this tale:

"A fire once broke out in a home and the neighbors came to help extinguish it. They started to carry out the furniture so that the fire would not spread. But in the bed, they found the householder fast asleep. In their excitement and haste, they lifted the bed and began carrying it out with the man in it, but when they came to the door, they found it was too narrow. They tried in every way, but they could not get the bed out.

"A bystander, watching their futile efforts, called out: 'Why don't you wake him up and save the man? Then you can take the bed out.'

"Knocking on the door," continued the Rabbi, "is not enough. He who is asleep may hear you and then go right back to sleep. You must knock until you are certain he is fully awake. The purpose of the *Selihot* Service is to arouse man's conscience so that he will repent of his sins and to do so, he must be fully awake. As Maimonides put it:

" 'Awake, you sleepers from your slumber and rouse you from your lethargy. Scrutinize your deeds and return in repentance. Remember your Creator, you who forget eternal truth in the trifles of the hour, who go astray all your years after vain illusions which can neither profit nor deliver. Look well into your souls and mend your ways and your actions; let each of you forsake his unworthy purpose, and return to God so that He may have mercy upon you.' "

RETURN TO GOD IN REPENTANCE

On one occasion the Chief Rabbi of Warsaw told his congregation why on the night of *Selihot* the *shamashim* (sextons)
should keep on knocking on every door in the community until people would open their doors and hear that it was time to
go to the Synagogue to recite the *Selihot* prayers of repentance.

"In The Song of Songs," said the Rabbi, "God is portrayed as
the Bridegroom and Israel as the Bride. The exile and dispersion of the Jews is interpreted to be a lovers' quarrel. Because
Israel has sinned, God is provoked and the Bride and Bridegroom are estranged. Each wants a reconciliation, but each is
waiting for the other to take the first step.

"God, the Bridegroom, says: 'Return, O Israel, to the Lord
your God' (Hosea 14:2).

"But Israel, the Bride, replies: 'Return us to Thee, O Lord,
and we shall return; renew our days as of old' (Lamentations
5:21).

"God then says. 'Return to Me and I will return to you'
(Malachi 3:7).

"But Israel counters: 'Arise, be our help and redeem us for
Thy mercy's sake' (Psalm 44:27).

"God pleads: 'Return to Me with all your heart' (Joel 2:12).

"But Israel asks: 'Arise and save us' (Jeremiah 2:27).

"God urges: 'Arise, shine, for your light has come' (Isaiah
60:1).

"But Israel insists: 'Arise, O God, judge the earth' (Psalm
82:8).

"Finally God agrees: 'I am My beloved's and My beloved is
Mine' (Song of Songs 6:3).

"And Israel responds: 'My beloved is mine and I am His'
(Song of Songs 2:16).

"Thus the reconciliation was effected. The first letter of the
Hebrew words *Ani l'dodi v'dodi li* 'I am My beloved's and My
beloved is Mine' spells the word *Elul,* the name of the month
preceding the High Holidays. Since God took the first step,
Israel promised every year, beginning with *Elul,* to open the
door to repentance. For this reason, the *shamashim* were to
knock on the doors before *Selihot* until the householders
open their doors and prepare to return to God in repentance."

THREE DAYS ROSH HASHANAH

The mystics tell us that one year there were three days of Rosh Hashanah. And how did this come about? This is what they say:

In the year 1944, the angels approached the Heavenly Throne and asked God: *Ematai Rosh Hashanah*—"When is Rosh Hashanah this year?"

And God replied: "Why do you ask Me? Remember, not I, but the *Bet Din shel matah* 'the Court on earth,' determines the date of Rosh Hashanah."

The angels then flew down to Jerusalem and heard the Rabbis of the *Bet Din* announce that Rosh Hashanah that year was to be observed on Monday and Tuesday. Thereupon they returned to heaven and began to prepare for the Day of Judgment. They brought out the records of every man on earth and placed them before the Heavenly Throne. Then they summoned the Prosecutor Satan; the Defender, the Archangel Gabriel; and witnesses to appear on the following Monday.

Early on Sunday morning, the day before Rosh Hashanah, one of the angels heard the chanting of the Rosh Hashanah prayer: *V'timlokh atah Adonai l'vadeh-kha* "Thou, O Lord, Thou alone, wilt rule over all Thy works on Mount Zion."

"Why today?" asked the angel. "This is Sunday. I heard the Rabbis announce that Rosh Hashanah will be observed tomorrow, Monday. Why do they chant this prayer today?"

The angel flew down to Jerusalem and to her great surprise, found all the shops open. Everyone was buying food and preparing for tomorrow's holiday. But again the angel heard the chanting of the Rosh Hashanah prayers. It seemed to come from a distance—from somewhere in Europe. But Europe was overrun by the Nazis. Who could be praying there?

The angel flew to Yugoslavia, but when she reached that country, the chanting seemed to come from some place farther away, perhaps Italy. In Italy, the voices sounded as if they came from Germany, the home of the Nazis!

The angel then flew over Germany past Munich, and here distinctly heard that the prayers were emanating from the Cathedral of Cologne. Upon entering the Cathedral, she saw the Bishop, but certainly the chanting did not come from him. Besides, the voices were children's voices! The angel continued to follow the sound, and came into a little room where two children dressed as altar boys were both chanting the Rosh Hashanah prayers. From them she learned that in order to save their lives, their parents had sent them to this Cathedral and they had promised to remember and observe all the Jewish holy days. Having no calendar and no contact with other Jews, they did not know the exact day of Rosh Hashanah. They assumed it was this day, Sunday.

The angel, greatly moved by the sight of these children and their devotion to the traditions of their people, flew directly to heaven to report the incident.

All the angels were deeply stirred. "When is Rosh Hashanah?" they asked each other. "Is it Monday, the day fixed by the Rabbis of Jerusalem, or is it today, the day fixed by the children in Cologne? What can be done about this? We cannot offend the Rabbis, and we cannot disappoint the children."

After a few moments of discussion, one of the angels spoke up: "I know what we'll do. We'll observe Rosh Hashanah three days this year." Without dissent, all the angels agreed.

When Satan, the Prosecutor heard this, he sneered:

"Absurd! I never heard of such a thing! Not the Rosh Hashanah set by the Rabbis, but the Rosh Hashanah set by the children?" And Satan did not appear before the Heavenly Throne that Sunday.

God, however, who considers sacred the feelings of all children, held Court without the Prosecutor, and the decrees issued from His Throne were the most favorable in centuries. He decreed the fall of Hitler and the restoration of Zion as a homeland for the Jewish people.

The mystics still believe that the reestablishment of the State of Israel was due in large measure to the loyalty and devotion of children.

AVINU MALKENU—OUR FATHER, OUR KING

In many Synagogues, the congregation chants aloud the last verse of the prayer, *Avinu Malkenu* "Our Father, our King," although there is a note in earlier editions of the Prayer Book that this verse is to be recited quietly. Why do congregations disregard that ancient practice and sing the verse out loud? And why was it originally recited in a low voice?

In this prayer of many verses, we ask for well-being, health, prosperity and peace. "Remove pestilence, sword, famine and captivity . . . Destroy the power of every oppressor . . . Send healing to the sick among Thy people . . . Inscribe us in the Book of Merit . . . Inscribe us in the Book of Happiness . . . Return us to Thee in perfect repentance . . . Forgive and pardon us."

We are asking God for the most precious things in life but when we conclude our list of requests, we sometimes feel like the villager who went to a supermarket and was overwhelmed by the variety of goods. He selected the choicest articles of food and placed them in a basket, but when he reached the cashier, he found that he had no money with which to pay for them. In a subdued voice, so that none might overhear, he asked the clerk to let him take these goods on credit and promised that in the near future he would pay for them.

Similarly, the worshiper asks God for all the blessings of life but, as he concludes his prayer, he realizes he does not have enough merit to compensate for all that he has requested. He therefore says in a hushed voice: "Our Father, our King, be gracious unto us and answer us for we are lacking in good deeds and we are unworthy. Deal Thou kindly with us and save us." In other words, he is saying: "Give us these blessings on credit and we will try to earn them in the coming year."

This has always been the general attitude until our generation. Now the Israeli can say: "We have accomplished much. We have cleared the land of malaria, planted trees, and converted deserts into gardens. We have built cities and schools. We have welcomed hundreds of thousands of homeless people. Our children have sacrificed their lives in the War of Independence."

And the Jews in America can say: "We have built Synagogues, Seminaries, Hospitals, Centers and Homes for the Aged, and we are helping our fellow Jews to rebuild Zion. We are establishing Colleges and Universities. We are participating in Community Chest campaigns and in civic and national causes. Because of these good deeds we need no longer lower our voices when we sing the last verse of the *Avinu Malkenu.*"

The words remain the same, but even though we change the mode of rendition, the text in itself is still significant. We must ever remain humble and realize that our work is not yet completed; there is much more to be done. As we face the New Year, we must resolve to continue our efforts on behalf of our people and all mankind so that we shall not appear unworthy before God when we ask for His blessings.

THE DAYS OF GOD'S LIGHT

When God created the sun and moon, the moon, wanting to be the only source of light, protested: "Why should two kings have to share the same crown?" For her arrogance, the moon was punished by being made smaller than the sun. She then complained: "Do I deserve such punishment simply because I asked a sensible question?"

"Very well," said God. "I shall give you the stars to shine with you at night." But the moon was still dissatisfied.

"You give the sun 365 days a year, and me only 355. Why should I have ten days less than the sun?" And to pacify the moon, God said:

"I will take away ten days from the sun for Myself. These shall be known as 'The Ten Days of Repentance.' They shall be My light. These ten days shall commence on Rosh Hashanah and end on the Day of Atonement. On Rosh Hashanah, when I judge man and the world, man shall have ten days in which to repent and improve his conduct. Man, who often lives in spiritual darkness, shall have My light to see the truth, the goodness, and the joy of life. To help him see by My light, he shall repeat morning and evening, during the High Holiday season, the words of the Psalmist: 'The Lord is my light and salvation, whom shall I fear? The Lord is the stronghold of my life, of whom shall I be afraid?' " (Psalm 27:1).

GOD EXTENDS HIS HAND

Ezekiel's vision of the Divine Chariot described in his first chapter has become the central theme of all Jewish esoteric literature, speculative theology and mysticism.

The chariot which Ezekiel saw was carried by four living creatures with human and animal features. Each had the face of a man in front, of a lion on the right, of an ox on the left, and of an eagle behind. . . . And they had the hands of a man under their wings on all four sides (1:8,10).

The word for "hand" in the text, is written *yod dalet vav*—literally "his hand"—but is read as if the *vav* were a *yod* which is the plural construct and means "the hands of" a man. The scholar Resh Lakish, accepting the written form "His hand," says it refers to God's hand. Others prefer to interpret the word literally as referring to a man's hand.

Symbolically, both interpretations suggest a profound concept. God's hand and man's hand meet under the wings of an animal. Man has animal instincts and often acts like an animal. How can he rise above his animal instincts? Only by extending his hand to God. And God then extends His hand to help him.

When man, regretting his transgression, says: "I have sinned. I am an animal and cannot control myself," let him stretch out his hand to God in repentance.

Thus we read in our High Holiday prayers: *Atah noten yad l'posh'im* "Thou, O Lord, givest Thy hand to transgressors and Thy right hand is stretched out to receive the penitent. Thou hast taught us to confess before Thee all our iniquities, so that we might withhold our hands from violence."

A NEW MEASURE OF SORROW IN THE KOL NIDRE

When the Nazis entered Wilna they began destroying the Synagogues. Although some Jews managed to save a few of the *Sifrè Torah,* they were forbidden to hold any public Service. Nevertheless, even at peril of their lives, they were determined to hold the Kol Nidre Service. A secret meeting-place was designated, and by word of mouth people were informed where the Service would take place. Shmuel, a pious Jew, was appointed to be the *Hazan* (Cantor). Someone had salvaged a single High Holiday Prayer Book, and the worshipers looked forward with great trepidation to this Service.

The morning before Kol Nidre, Shmuel's wife Sarah, who went out to look for food, was seized by the Gestapo and carried off to a concentration camp. When she did not return, Shmuel and his little son Hezkel, became anxious. The child began crying and saying: "I'm hungry. Where's Mother?" His father tried in vain to calm him and then went out to search for his wife. When he learned what had happened, he returned home and found Hezkel still crying. "Where's Mother? I'm hungry," he sobbed.

It was getting late, and the people were already assembled for the Kol Nidre, but Shmuel was too distressed to conduct the Service. Two of the congregation came to summon him but when they heard what had happened, they grieved with him.

"We know how you feel," they said, "but everyone is waiting for the Kol Nidre. You are the only one who has a *Mahzor* (Prayer Book) and who knows best how to chant. These people came at the risk of their lives and they'll be terribly disappointed if you are not there to officiate."

Shmuel took his son by the hand and went to the hideout where Jews gathered to pray. He put on his *tallit,* opened the Prayer Book and was about to chant when Hezkel again burst out crying: "Where's Mother? I'm hungry."

Tears welled in Shmuel's eyes; his voice broke and became husky. He lifted Hezkel up on the improvised pulpit and, with his arm around his son, announced to the congregation:

"Forgive me. I'm sorry. I cannot be your *Hazan* tonight."

Shimon Baer, the oldest among them, immediately stepped up to the pulpit, took Shmuel's Prayer Book and *tallit,* and the congregation, weeping for Shmuel and all the others who had that year become victims of the cruel Nazis, rose as one and together with Shimon Baer, chanted the Kol Nidre, expressing their profound grief in the age-old melody that this year had taken on more measures of sorrow.

ONE PEOPLE UNITED

Mendele of Zakrochen, who had recently come to Jerusalem from a concentration camp, asked permission of the Curator to officiate at the Kol Nidre Service in the Synagogue on Mount Zion. Most of his friends had died in the gas chambers and in their memory he wanted to offer the prayers near the Chamber of Destruction. His request was granted, but when he put on his *tallit* and *kittel* before the Service, Shabbati, a Sephardic Jew, approached him.

"Excuse me," he said. "I always conduct the Service here."

Perturbed, Mendele explained: "The Curator gave me permission. I represent the six million Jews who were killed, and I would like to conduct the Kol Nidre Service in their memory."

But Shabbati argued: "As a sixth generation Israeli, I represent all the generations who have lived in the Holy Land."

An argument ensued and one of the bystanders suggested that the Curator should decide between them. The Curator was in a quandary. Shabbati had never been officially authorized to conduct the Services, but every Sabbath when it was time to pray, he went to the pulpit and no one had ever questioned his right. The Curator did not know how to resolve the issue.

"Who am I to decide who is entitled to officiate at this Service—the one who represents the six million who were killed, or the one who represents the six generations who have lived in the Holy Land?" he asked himself.

Mendele and Shabbati continued the argument until it was time to commence the Service. Then they turned to the Curator and asked his decision.

And the Curator said: "Both of you are entitled to conduct the Service. Let both of you stand side by side and officiate together."

Then a strange thing happened. Here were two Jews, one Sephardic and the other Ashkenazic; their voices were different and their melodies and pronunciations were different. Yet, when they chanted the Kol Nidre, the people heard only one voice and one melody.

The same is true of all in Israel. Jews speaking many different languages and dialects have come from many countries of the world, and thus represent many varied cultures and backgrounds. But in Israel they are all united. They speak in one voice. One language, Hebrew, unites all the people; one hope and one goal weld the heterogeneous groups into a unified community.

THE SONG OF THE ANGELS

The *Shema*—that sublime declaration of the unity of God: "Hear, O Israel, the Lord our God, the Lord is One!"—is followed by the verse *Barukh Shem* "Praised be His glorious sovereign Name forever and ever." Throughout the year this second verse, usually printed in prayer books in smaller type than the *Shema,* is read silently by tradition-observing Jews. On Kol Nidre Night, however, and before the Shofar is sounded at the end of the Yom Kippur Service, the worshipers recite aloud the second verse, *Barukh Shem.*

The same verse is proclaimed aloud three times on Yom Kippur Day during the *Avodah Service* which minutely describes the awe-inspiring atonement ritual that took place in the Temple at Jerusalem:

"When the Priests and the people who stood in the Court heard the revered Name of God pronounced by the High Priest in holiness and purity, they knelt and prostrated themselves, and in gratitude to God, fell on their faces and said: 'Praised be His glorious sovereign Name forever and ever.' "

Why is this verse *Barukh Shem* read silently throughout the year except on the Day of Atonement when it is intoned aloud?

There is an ancient legend that this verse was once exclusively the song of angels. But when Moses was for forty days on Mount Sinai in order to receive the Torah and overheard the song, he liked it so well that he learned it and taught it to his people. When the angels heard the Children of Israel singing their song, they complained to God that Moses had appropriated it. Thereupon God decided that the Children of Israel may recite it quietly throughout the year, except on Kol Nidre Night and Yom Kippur when they may chant it aloud.

But when the angels heard the Children of Israel singing their song on Kol Nidre Night and on Yom Kippur, they again complained to God.

And God said: "On this day, the Children of Israel are fervently praying in their Synagogues. Clothed in white, they abstain from food and drink and are ethereal like the angels; therefore, on Yom Kippur they are entitled to sing your song *Barukh Shem*."

This most Holy Day, when Jews together with the angels praised God's Name, is a time to pray that through repentance, prayer and deeds of kindness, the people on earth shall attain the spiritual heights of the angels throughout the year.

WHAT ABOUT TOMORROW?

In a city in eastern Europe, on the Day of Atonement, the Synagogue was crowded with worshipers. Everyone was imbued with lofty sentiments of forgiveness, and deeply moved and inspired by the Rabbi and Cantor. Just before the Shofar was to be sounded at the conclusion of the Ne'ilah, the Rabbi fainted. When he was revived he was asked: "What happened?" And the Rabbi said: "I heard a voice repeating: 'How nice! How fine! How good!' It must have been Satan who was saying this."

"Satan!" the people exclaimed. "Satan would never say 'How nice! How fine! How good!'"

But the Rabbi explained that Satan uttered these words sarcastically. "The Talmud tells us," he said, "that Satan is busy every day except on the Day of Atonement. The numerical value of the Hebrew letters *heh, sin, tet* and *nun* in the word *ha-Satan* is 364, and indicates that Satan is active every day of the year except *one*.

"On that one day, Yom Kippur," continued the Rabbi, "Satan can neither make a false accusation against the Jews, nor speak ill of them, nor can he tempt them. So he just laughs and says: 'How nice! How fine! How good today! They are in the Synagogue all day. They fast and pray. Yesterday before Kol Nidre they asked pardon of all whom they had wronged. Now they repent their misdeeds and ask God to forgive them. All is love and peace in their hearts. They strive for holiness and to a certain degree approach it. How good and easy it is for them today! *But what about tomorrow?* Will they stay tomorrow on the same lofty plateau they have reached today?'

"When I heard Satan mocking us, I was so horrified that I fainted."

The Rabbi turned to the congregation. "What *will* happen tomorrow?" he asked. "Unless we retain the High Holiday spirit during the entire coming year, our prayers will all have been in vain. The inspiration of the sacred season now drawing to a close must be an incentive to greater devotion to Torah, to our people and to Zion. Then we shall remain all the days of the year on the lofty plateau we have reached this day, and if Satan tries to entice us on any of his 364 days, we shall certainly have the will power to overcome temptation.

THE SILENT ALEPH

The Kabalists tell us that at one time the Hebrew word for "sin" was *san* which consists of two letters, *samekh* and *nun*. The *samekh* is for the word *sam* "poison" and the letter *nun* is for *nahash* "snake." Thus sin was personified as "poisonous snake."

On one occasion, the Kabalists say that Satan entered into a dispute with God.

"You want man to have freedom of choice," Satan claimed. "You gave him both good and evil inclinations. Isn't character strengthened when man faces temptation and overcomes it? But when man confronts sin as a 'poisonous snake,' he will not overcome temptation because he will be frightened and run away."

God realized the validity of Satan's remarks and said: "I will disguise the word for 'sin' by using the *at bash* system.* Instead of *samekh nun* which personifies 'poisonous snake' I will substitute the letters *het* and *tet*. Man will no longer recognize this new word for 'sin' and he will then be able to exercise freedom of choice. I will make a slight addition, however; I will add My letter *aleph* to the letters *het* and *tet*. Thus the word for 'sin' will be spelled *het tet aleph*. When man is tempted to sin, on hearing My letter *aleph* pronounced, he will remember that he is created in My image and will therefore be inclined to overcome temptation."

But Satan was still dissatisfied. "That would be unfair," he said. "When man hears Your letter *aleph* he will certainly not have freedom of choice. You should take the *aleph* out of the word 'sin.' "

And God replied: "Once My letter is given I cannot take it away but, to satisfy you, My letter shall be silent and not pronounced."

Satan reluctantly agreed and thus the *aleph* in the Hebrew word for "sin" is silent.

Whenever man is tempted to do wrong, he should remember that though silent, God is standing near and hopes that man will be strong enough to resist every evil impulse.

---

* For *aleph*, the first letter of the alphabet, the last letter *tav* is substituted. For *bet*, the second letter, the penultimate letter *shin* is substituted, etc.

REMOVE THE OLD GARMENTS

When the High Priest performed the *Avodah Service,* he changed his garments four times and before making each change, he had to remove the garments he was already wearing.

A peasant came to the city for the first time and everyone stared at him because his garments were shabby and strange. Impressed with the clothes he saw others wearing, he went into a store and bought a new suit. But when he returned home and put on the suit, it did not fit. Returning to the store, he made his complaint.

"That suit you sold me does not fit."

The clerk laughed. "Of course it does not fit! You put on the new garment over your old clothes! You have to take off the old before you can put on the new."

Thus it is with the New Year. We cannot enjoy a new year, enter upon a new phase of life, and acquire a new outlook unless we first get rid of our old and outworn habits of thinking and acting. We must first remove the old habits of selfishness, vanity and greed before we can change to a new and better mode of life.

We read in the Book of Zechariah (3:3,4) that Joshua was clothed in filthy garments and stood before the angel. And the angel said to those who stood before him: "Remove the filthy garments from him." And to Joshua he said: "Behold, I have taken away your iniquity and I will clothe you with clean robes."

THE LIGHT THAT SHINES FOR US

Many years ago, Safed in Palestine was governed by a ruler unfriendly to the Jews. When he found that they were studying Torah at night by candlelight, he decreed that no light should be lit.

"God made the sun to shine by day," he said, "and does not desire any light at night."

The Jews therefore studied Torah by day but many, defying the decree, studied by candlelight in their cellars, where they might not be detected. Fortunately, evening services in the Synagogue were brief and held just prior to sunset. The problem was, what to do on Kol Nidre Night when the Service is long. On Kol Nidre Night, moreover, Synagogues are brightly illuminated. Light is symbolic of hope and faith.

On the Kol Nidre Night after the decree was issued, when the Jews assembled in their Synagogue, they were downcast because for the first time they were forced to hold the Service without lights. But, without any warning, thousands of fireflies flew inside the building and filled the Synagogue with light.

When the ruler of Safed heard that the Synagogue was illuminated, he summoned his soldiers to go to the Synagogue and take the Jews into custody. But the Service had just concluded when he and his soldiers arrived.

The ruler angrily turned to the Rabbi. "Who lit the lights?" he demanded.

"No one lit the lights," replied the Rabbi. "You can see for yourself. It came from the fireflies on the ceiling. The same God who you say does not desire any light at night, has sent His fireflies to shine for us."

The ruler was astounded.

"I see that your God wants you to have light at night," he said. "But tell me, why did He select this particular night?"

"Because on Kol Nidre Night we light candles in memory of
our departed," explained the Rabbi. "We believe that the souls
of our parents and all our dear ones who have gone to their
eternal reward are here with us in the Synagogue. You forbade
us to light candles; therefore the fireflies supplied the light that
shines for us on this night. As we read in Proverbs 20:27, 'The
soul of man is the light of the Eternal.' "

Other Comments on Yom Kippur

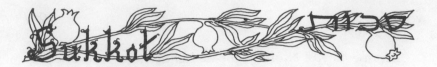

YOUR GUESTS GRACE THE SUKKAH

The children of Rabbi Hayim of Tzans helped their father erect a *Sukkah*. But when they asked him for money to buy the necessary decorations for it, the Rabbi told them to come back later. In the meantime three destitute men came to see him and the Rabbi gave them all the money in his purse. When later his children again asked him for money to buy decorations for the *Sukkah,* he said: "I'm sorry, children. I have no money."

"But what about the adornment of the *Sukkah?*" they asked.

"Oh, I have already prepared the decorations," the Rabbi replied.

The children looked into the *Sukkah,* but it was bare.

"There are no decorations. There is nothing there," they said.

"You will soon see them," answered their father.

At mealtime, the same three destitute men, now wearing new clothes, came in and were welcomed by the Rabbi who whispered to his children:

"These guests are the decorations of the *Sukkah.*" The children were puzzled, but not wishing to appear lacking in good manners, they said nothing. After the guests left, the Rabbi explained:

"In the Bible, wherever the word Sukkot appears, it is written without the letter *vav* and this suggests that something is missing. The *Sukkah* by itself is not complete. There is something lacking. It is only complete when we bring into it kindness and hospitality. Then it is properly decorated. We have the beautiful traditional custom of *ushpizin,* inviting into the *Sukkah* 'spiritual guests': Abraham, Isaac, Jacob, Joseph, Moses, Aaron and David. But besides these, we should invite human guests, not only friends and dear ones, but also the lonely and forlorn. Only then can the Sukkot Festival be a truly joyful occasion."

TWO WHO SIGH ON SUKKOT

The celebration of Sukkot in Jerusalem is a highly colorful and joyous occasion and there is much singing and dancing, especially on Simhat Torah. We are told in Hasidic literature that in the midst of all these festivities, the most pious Jews can hear sighing. But who can be sighing on the Festival of which the Bible says: "You shall be altogether joyful?" (Deuteronomy 16:15).

The Hasidim say that both King David and God are sighing. Why does King David sigh? Because he sees everyone erecting a *Sukkah*, the symbol of peace. *Ufros alenu sukkat shlomekha* "Spread over us Thy tabernacle of peace." Yet where is there peace in this world? When will people help to realize the prayer in the *Birkat Hamazon: Haraha'man hu yakim lanu el Sukkat David hanofelet* "May the All-merciful God restore for us the fallen Tabernacle of King David?"

And why is God sighing? He sighs when He sees Jews leaving the *Sukkah* and going into their homes. After the Festival, where will the *Shekhinah* "God's Spirit" be found? Will it be in their homes? Will every home be an altar and every heart inclined to receive it? Will God's Spirit be found in the schools, in the seats of government, in the market place, in man's relations with his fellow men?

The absence of world peace for which David sighs, may well be because God's Spirit has not been taken into our midst. When the *Shekhinah* shall become a dynamic force in our daily living, motivating every field of human endeavor—only then shall the world achieve stability and know the peace for which both God and David sigh.

Other Comment on Sukkot

REJOICE IN YOUR FESTIVAL, page 191

A FESTIVAL FOR OURSELVES

The Bible tells us that we are to observe the Festival of Sukkot for seven days (Deuteronomy 16:13). But why is *Shemini Atzeret,* an eighth day also required?

Sukkot has its universal aspect. On the first day of Sukkot, we read in the *Haftarah* from the Book of Zechariah (14:16):

"It shall come to pass that everyone who is left of all the nations that fought against Jerusalem, will go up from year to year to worship the King, the Lord of hosts, and to observe the Feast of Sukkot."

In Biblical times, during the Sukkot Festival, it was the custom to sacrifice seventy animals in the Temple on behalf of the well-being and peace of the seventy nations of the then known world. And on Mount Zion, in our day, seventy candles are lit on Sukkot and a special prayer is recited for the well-being of all the nations of the world:

"We pray to Thee, O Lord, from Jerusalem, the city of peace, and from Mount Zion, the sanctuary of Thy glory. Have mercy on Thy world, on all lands and all peoples, and protect them from war which will destroy mankind. O Sovereign of peace, mayest Thou speedily instill Thy spirit of peace and brotherhood in the hearts of all peoples, so that they may make a covenant of peace for all time, even as Thou didst foretell through the words of Thy Prophets in the vision of the End of Days."

Now, as to *Shemini Atzeret,* the eighth day, there is a legend that God says to the Children of Israel: "For seven days you have concerned yourselves with the well-being of all peoples. This is altogether laudable, but you must not neglect your own needs. Therefore pause and add one day to the Sukkot Festival, and call it *Shemini Atzeret* 'the Eighth Day of Assembly.' "

The first three Hebrew letters of *Atzeret* are *ayin, tzadik* and *resh* which make up the word *atzer* "to halt or stop temporarily." That is to say "Halt and pause for one day to consider your own needs, your own spiritual welfare and the Torah which God has given to you. On the eighth day, rejoice with the Torah.* Observe a Yizkor Service in remembrance of your dear departed and meditate upon their lives, ideals and sacrifices. It is always commendable to concern yourselves with the problems of humanity, but set aside this one day in order to concentrate upon your own welfare."

---

* In Israel and in some other lands, Simhat Torah takes place on *Shemini Atzeret.*

 Simhat Torah שמחת תורה

IS THE TORAH REJOICING WITH YOU?

A Rabbi saw Shmuel singing, dancing and rejoicing with the pious men in the Torah procession on Simhat Torah.

"I never saw you studying the Torah or observing the *mitzvot*," said the Rabbi. "Why are you rejoicing? Is it really your *simha*?"

"When my brother's son was married," said Shmuel, "without an invitation I came to his *simha*. The Jews here are my brothers. I have a right to come to their *simha*."

"I am delighted that you feel that way," said the Rabbi. "It is good to see you rejoicing with the Torah. But is the Torah rejoicing with you?"

Shmuel took the hint and thereafter began to study the Torah and observe its teachings.

FAITH IS RECIPROCAL

Rabbi Shlomo David Kahana, when he was Chief Rabbi of Warsaw, maintained a Synagogue in his home. One evening while the worshipers were carrying the Scrolls of the Torah on Simhat Torah, Nazis armed with weapons, broke into the Synagogue, beat the Jews and threw down their *Sifre Torah*. The Jews did not disperse; neither did they despair. On the contrary, as soon as the Nazis left, they picked up their Torahs and joyfully resumed their *hakafah* "procession."

When the Lubavitcher Rabbi heard of this incident, he said: "*Hakafah* means not only procession but also to trust or to extend credit. Now I understand why Simhat Torah comes so soon after Yom Kippur. God trusts His people and extends them credit. Shortly after Yom Kippur, when one's fate for the coming year is sealed, God ordained Simhat Torah, a day of joy, to indicate that He had faith that the Children of Israel will so conduct themselves as to be worthy of the joy in store for them. I see now that this trust is reciprocal. Not only does God trust His people but His people trust Him. We may well ask: 'How can Jews rejoice with the Torah and retain their faith in God when the Nazis are so barbaric?' The answer is that despite persecutions, the Jews carry their Torahs in procession on Simhat Torah and reaffirm their faith that God will yet inspire men to achieve a world free from fear, hatred and violence. Thus God not only trusts His people, but His people trust Him."

The establishment of the State of Israel vindicates the Jew's faith in God. The Jew is an eternal optimist. He has faith that the day will yet come when justice and peace will prevail for all mankind.

THE TORAH CARRIES US

At a Simhat Torah celebration, an old man was carrying a large *Sefer Torah* in the procession, when someone asked him:

"Isn't the Torah too heavy for you? You are old and feeble and the Torah is so heavy."

"On the contrary," the old man replied. "I chose to carry the largest Scroll because we are told: *Ha-Torah nosah et no-se-eha* 'The Torah carries those who hold it aloft.' The heavier it is, the easier it is for the Torah to carry me."

When the Jews were herded in the Warsaw ghetto, they were told that if they did not run they would be beaten. A man of seventy, bent and infirm, was leading his grandchild by the hand. As they ran, the child fell and bruised his leg. When he arose he could only limp along. Fearing that the Nazis would club the boy, the old man placed him on his shoulder and forced himself to keep running.

"What are you doing?" someone asked. "You can hardly run yourself. You are old and weak. How can you carry the child on your shoulder?"

"How wrong you are!" the old man replied. "I'm not carrying the child; the child is carrying me. Were it not for him, I would not be able to take a step."

When we perform a *mitzvah* of any kind, that *mitzvah* will sustain us. When we pursue a worthy goal or purpose, that goal or purpose uplifts us; no task is too difficult or impossible.

THE TORAH UPRAISED

Among the Torah Scrolls carried in the joyous Mount Zion procession on Simhat Torah, there is one known by the unusual name, "The Torah Upraised." Although extremely heavy, this Torah is held aloft and unrolled so that everyone in the congregation may behold its sacred script. This Torah has a poignant history.

During the week of Sukkot, a Nazi Commissar arrived with his soldiers at the town of Prushnitz in Poland and drove out all the Jews. The brutal Storm Troopers set the Synagogue afire, dragged the Jews out of their homes, and forced them to run to the deportation centers whence they were hauled off to a concentration camp.

The older people were soon exhausted, their hearts overstrained. Whoever collapsed was shot.

When the Synagogue was set ablaze, Reb Gedaliah the sexton, risked his life in order to rescue a *Sefer Torah* from the flames. A Storm Trooper caught him and forced him to run with the holy Scroll toward the deportation depot. Suddenly Reb Gedaliah stumbled and the Torah dropped to the ground.

Old Baruch, running beside him, picked up the holy Scroll, but a friend called to him:

"Give it to me. You're old and feeble. You're not strong enough to run with the *Sefer Torah*."

"You're mistaken," replied Baruch. "The Torah is not too heavy for me. It is my Tree of Life. As long as I hold it aloft it sustains and strengthens me."

With the Torah, Baruch ran all the way to the depot and concealed it in a dark corner under his bunk. In all these years in the concentration camp, he found his solace and hope in that Torah.

When he was liberated, he was convinced that it was the Torah that had kept him alive. He took the *Sefer Torah* with him when later he sailed for Israel and presented it to the Curator of Mount Zion. And every year on Simhat Torah, that same Torah is carried in the procession high above all the others and is called "The Torah Upraised."

Hanukkah   חנוכה

THE LITTLE CANDLES

On Hanukkah, in Israeli hotels and public buildings, and in many Jewish institutions throughout the world, large candles are lit or menorahs are illuminated by electricity or neon lights. In striking contrast, the Hanukkah candles kindled in the menorah on Mount Zion are small, similar to those traditionally used for centuries in Jewish homes. Our ancestors used small candles, not because of poverty—they would have found the means to buy large candles if they were essential—but because these lesser lights taught a significant truth.

One of the miracles of Hanukkah was that the small cruse of oil, enough for but one night's illumination, burned for eight days. The small candles therefore suggest that great size and quantity are not always the deciding factor; the feeble and few may have tremendous potentiality and power. This is emphasized in the *Al Hanisim* prayer: "Thou, O Lord, didst deliver the many into the hands of the few, the strong into the hands of the weak."

Shakespeare recognized the potency of the small, good deed: "How far that little candle throws its beams! So shines a good deed in a naughty world." Character is developed by the small acts that a man performs every day.

Not the great countries of the world but the Holy Land, a territory of insignificant size, produced the Bible, gave birth to the great religions of the world, and brought forth the valiant Prophets who have endowed humanity with the ideals of kindness, justice and peace. In comparison with most compendiums and encyclopedias, the Bible is small, but it has exerted incalculable influence upon the whole world.

The Jewish people are few in number, but they have given the world some of the greatest teachers, philosophers, scientists, philanthropists, artists, novelists, playwrights and Nobel Prize winners.

The Eternal Light which burns in every Synagogue is small, but it is a constant reminder of the great truths so direly needed in the world today. Israel is a comparatively small country, but its achievements are already great and significant.

As we read in the Prophetical portion on the Sabbath of Hanukkah; "Not by might, nor by power, but by My spirit, says the Lord of hosts" (Zechariah 4:6).

THE MENORAH ON THE THRESHOLD

History tells us that Antiochus forbade the Jews to study Torah or to observe any of the Jewish traditions. According to a midrash, not only were the Jews to remove from their doorposts the *mezuzah* containing the Biblical passage, Deuteronomy 6:4-9, inscribed on parchment, but they were also to write on their doors: *En li helek venahalah b'elohay Yisrael* "I have no interest in the God of Israel."

The Jews were in a quandary. If they wrote these words it would mean that they were forsaking their God and their religion. If they did not write them, the Syrians would most certainly persecute them. The faithful solved their dilemma by removing their doors and leaving open their dwellings. The Hanukkah menorah was therefore placed on the threshold. Although Hanukkah occurs during the rainy and windy season, we are told by the mystics that the menorah prevented the rain and wind from entering the home. God protected them, they say, so that neither rain nor cold winds nor thieves could enter their homes. When victory came and the Maccabees defeated the Syrians, in order to commemorate this miracle of God's protection, the Jews placed the Hanukkah menorah on the threshold and left the door open.

The *Shulhan Arukh* tells us that on Hanukkah the Jew is to walk between the *mezuzah* on the right jamb of the door and the menorah on the left. The light of the menorah shines on the *mezuzah* in order to indicate that the light of God's teachings is to illumine our lives. "The Lord is my light and salvation; whom shall I fear?" (Psalm 27:1).

THE FIRST VICTORY FOR RELIGIOUS LIBERTY

Hanukkah recalls several great miracles. When the Maccabees defeated the Syrians and wanted to rededicate the Temple polluted by the enemy, they found a small cruse of oil which they thought sufficient for only one day's illumination. But lo and behold!—the oil burned for eight days.

The victory of the few and weak over the many and mighty was another miracle. But perhaps the greatest miracle of all occurred when Mattathias the Priest, revolting against Antiochus, was joined by his children. His five sons, especially Judah, were all heroes and they inspired their followers to victory. The prayer *Al Hanisim* specifically mentions them: *Bimay Mattityahu . . . uvanav* "In the days of Mattathias . . . and his sons." Mattathias might have issued the call to defy the enemy, but his might have been a voice crying in the wilderness and his children might have been indifferent to the call. The unity of the whole family defeated organized tyranny.

The strength of the Jew is best perceived whenever the older and younger generations see eye to eye with reference to their problems and needs. In the very beginning of Jewish history, Abraham and Isaac walked together, *Vayelkhu sh'nehem yahdav* "Father and son walked together" (Genesis 22:6). The survival of the Jew may be partially attributed to the harmony existing between parents and children.

Had the children of Mattathias refused to follow their father, the Jews would have been defeated, and there would have been no Judaism, no Bible, no Christianity and no Mohammedanism.

The victory of the Maccabees, due in no small measure to the loyalty and heroism of the sons of Mattathias, was one of the decisive triumphs in world history; the first victory for religious freedom and for the right of a people to maintain its own identity and individuality.

THE WORD HANUKKAH

There are several explanations for the word Hanukkah. It is derived from the Hebrew word meaning "dedication." The enemy had defiled the Temple by offering pagan sacrifices on the altar of God. But the victorious Maccabees cleansed the Temple and rededicated it to God. The same term *Hanukkat Habayit* is used in dedicating a home or institution.

The word Hanukkah can be read: *Hanu kof heh* "They rested on the twenty-fifth day" because the Maccabees ceased fighting on the twenty-fifth day of Kislev.

There are some who see in the word Hanukkah, the name Hannah. It was Hannah and her seven sons who, by refusing to bow down to the idols, set the example of devotion to God and of self-sacrifice for their religion.

Other Comments on Hanukkah

NOT BY MIGHT . . . BUT BY MY SPIRIT, page 49

THE FEW SHALL PREVAIL, page 50

THE TREES THAT BOW

Tu Bishevat, the fifteenth day of the month of *Shevat,* known as The New Year of the Trees, is the Jewish Arbor Day, when trees are planted all over Israel. And on Mount Zion there are some old bent trees about which there is a fanciful tale.

When the Temple was destroyed and the Jews were exiled, all living things on earth wanted to die together with the House of God. The sun was unwilling to shine; the moon did not want to appear at night; the stars had no desire to illumine the heavens; nothing wanted to live; the whole world went into mourning. But from heaven there came a cry:

"Would you ruin God's beautiful world? Why do you despair? Have patience. All is not lost. The Jews shall return. The Temple shall be rebuilt, and the Children of Israel will again flourish."

The trees on Mount Zion most especially wanted to be swallowed up by the earth. The Temple was burning; why should they continue to grow? Their branches drooped and were about to fall to the ground. Then a voice from heaven cried out again:

"You trees! Would you ruin God's beautiful world? Grow! Put forth your branches and live! Do not wither and fade into the earth!"

The trees tried to raise their branches and gaze upward into the sun but, when they saw the Temple in flames and their beloved people driven into exile, they could no longer stand upright and their heads again bent low.

"How can we stand erect when the heads of our people are bowed in grief?" they cried. "We shall await the redemption of our people." And to this very day they have remained bowed low in mourning.

Before the Jewish State was declared, the heads of the trees were so low they seemed to be touching the ground. Since then, they have grown straighter, but their heads are still bowed because they still await the ingathering of all the Jews who continue to suffer exile. Then they will again stand erect and raise their heads to the sun.

THE BIRDS FIND REFUGE

Tu Bishevat, the beginning of Spring in Israel, when flowers appear and trees are planted, always occurs a few days before or after *Shabbat Shirah,* the Sabbath of Song, when the Song of Moses is read (Exodus 15:1-18). When trees bud and blossom, the birds begin to sing. "The flowers appear in the land; the time of singing has come" (Song of Songs 2:12).

We are told that when the birds were first created, they had no place to rest. They could only fly around in the air; therefore they appealed to God:

"Everyone has a place to live. Man builds a home; the beasts have their dens. In the air we have no place on which to set our feet."

The trees at that time grew close to the ground and when they heard the plea of the birds, they called up to them:

"Come down to us. We will provide a home for you."

God was so pleased with their willingness to help, that he made the trees grow tall with spreading branches so that birds could find shelter and build their nests on them. For this reason, when trees begin to bud and blossom, the birds begin singing in gratitude.

Thus do the homeless rejoice when we provide homes for them, and by so doing we bring cheer into our own lives and into the world at large.

TREES AND JUSTICE

On *Tu Bishevat,* Jews in Israel plant trees, and the mystics believe that because the righteous man is likened to a tree (Psalm 1:3), these trees play a role in bringing justice to the world.

There is a folk tale about the great poet, Ibn Gabirol of Spain, a favorite of the King and his court. Don Pedro, a noble-man who came often to the King's palace, was extremely jealous of Ibn Gabirol's popularity. One day, Don Pedro invited Ibn Gabirol to a celebration in his home, but when the poet arrived, there were no other guests present. He waited for someone to appear when suddenly Don Pedro entered and without warning fell upon him and slew him.

When the poet, greatly beloved by all the people, no longer came to any of the court functions, everybody was mystified. And his absence was especially noted at the King's celebrations where, to everyone's delight, he would always read his poetry.

"What has happened to the court poet?" asked the nobles. "Is he ill?"

Weeks passed, but the mystery of Ibn Gabirol's disappearance remained unsolved. An investigation followed, and the King inquired of all Ibn Gabirol's neighbors and friends, but no one knew where he was.

One day, someone informed the King that he heard Don Pedro invite the poet to his home; perhaps he could give some information about Ibn Gabirol.

The King summoned Don Pedro and asked about the poet.

"I have not seen or heard from him," said Don Pedro.

For several more weeks the search continued and then the King decided to visit Don Pedro, who received His Majesty in his garden. The King observed that one of the trees was taller, more beautiful, better developed and gave forth more fragrance than all the rest.

"Where did you get this tree?" asked the King. "It's beautiful! It's different from all the others and has more leaves, flowers and branches. You must have given it special care to have it flourish so well."

Don Pedro paled. "That tree came from a place where special trees are grown," he said. "I saw it on my travels and brought it here to Spain so that its spreading branches and beautiful blossoms should grace my garden."

The King examined the tree again and again. "You are fortunate to have a tree like this. It makes your garden unique."

Many days passed, but the King could not forget Don Pedro's tree. The more he thought about it, the more beautiful it seemed in his mind's eye.

"I must see that tree once more," he said. And he again visited Don Pedro in his garden. This time he took with him two of his favorite dogs. He walked over to the tree and greatly admired it.

"Tell me, where did you say you got that tree? I would like to get one like it."

"I don't know where you can get one," Don Pedro replied. "I planted it years ago as a sapling."

The King's eyes narrowed. "Planted it as a sapling?"

"Yes, my brother had two, and he gave me one."

The King was a wise man, and he knew Don Pedro was not telling the truth because this was an altogether new story. There must be some mystery about that tree.

"I want a tree just like that one," he repeated, "and I am going to search the world over until I find one." At that moment, the King's dogs began barking and digging around the tree. "You see, even my dogs like this tree," said the King.

The dogs went on barking and digging and Don Pedro grew paler and paler.

"They will dig into the roots, Your Majesty!" he cried out. "They will ruin my tree." And he began to throw back the soil which the dogs had dug up.

The dogs had never barked so furiously, and they dug up more earth than Don Pedro could ever throw back. Suddenly, the King saw something protruding from the shallow earth.

"What's that?" he asked. The terrified Don Pedro began to stammer.

"That—that is a scarecrow—I—I decided to destroy."

"A scarecrow? A strange place to bury a scarecrow! Dig it up and let me see."

Don Pedro was paralyzed with fright; his eyes bulged in his head and he made no move to dig up the scarecrow.

But the King's dogs went on digging and before long they dug up the body of a man!

The King gasped. "Ibn Gabirol!" He turned on Don Pedro. "You—you killed Ibn Gabirol and buried him under this tree! You thought no one would ever discover your crime. This tree bears the blossoms of the poet and is fertilized by his blood. Justice will be done! You who took his life shall be hanged in your own garden near the tree where you buried the beloved Ibn Gabirol!"

The following day, Don Pedro paid with his life for his crime, and thus the tree played a part in bringing about justice in the world.

THE PRAYING TREES

We Jews, in the conviction that prayer sustains the world, pray daily for our people and for the peace of all mankind. There is an old legend that when the Temple was destroyed and the Jews exiled, the angels in heaven were aghast.

"Who will now pray for the world?" they cried.

To this the trees replied: "We will pray." And immediately they began praying.

Why does this legend say that trees will pray? Because according to ancient custom in the Holy Land, whenever a child was born, a tree was planted and became the symbol of that child.

The Bible asks: "Is the tree of the field like man?" (Deuteronomy 20:19). And tradition has it that the tree *is* like man (Psalm 1:3), that the tree reflects the life of the one for whom it was planted at his birth. When he performs good deeds, the tree flourishes and produces abundantly; when he is joyous the tree gaily sways in the breeze; when he is grief-stricken, the tree's branches droop; when he is ill, the tree begins to wither. Thus the tree reflects man's life.

This, we are told, applied especially to the Priests in ancient Jerusalem. When they were born, their parents planted trees. And when the Priests sang, the trees sang; when the Priests chanted prayers, the trees rustled their leaves; when the Temple was besieged and the Priests chanted dirges, the trees swayed and joined in mournful elegy.

Before the torch was laid to the Temple, the High Priest, crushed with grief, called out to the priesthood:

"What shall we do? Our Temple will be destroyed and our people will be scattered to the four corners of the world. We cannot remain here while our people go into exile. But if we leave with them, who shall pray for them in our absence? Who shall pray for our people and for the peace of the world?"

The High Priest came to Mount Zion and, leaning against the tree that his father had planted for him when he was born, cried out in anguish:

"Oh, who will pray for us? There will be no one here to pray to God if we go into exile with our people. What can we do? What shall we do?"

Suddenly, he heard a rustling; a breeze stirred the leaves of the trees, and they trembled. The High Priest listened and understood.

"The trees! *They* will remain here and take our place. *They* will pray for the people in our stead."

Some of the Priests went into exile with their people while others were slain by the enemy. But to this day, in place of the Temple priesthood, the trees on Mount Zion stand with heads bowed in prayer.

This secret of the Jewish people is one which their enemies can never understand. They have been exiled and driven from country to country, but the trees on Mount Zion which have remained there, still cry out:

"We stand forever for the men, women and children who were driven out, and we shall remain here to pray until all our exiles return."

Whenever Jews anywhere are humiliated, broken and forced to endure tragedy, the trees on Mount Zion can be heard even now, sighing and praying for the redemption of the Children of Israel.

HOW THE BIRDS BROUGHT JUSTICE

Tu Bishevat, Jewish Arbor Day, is observed a few days before or after *Shabbat Shirah* when the Song of Moses is read (Exodus 15:1-18). On this Sabbath it is customary to scatter crumbs to the birds. There is a story told of how the birds in the trees once brought about justice in Galilee.

In Safed there lived a poet and mystic, Shlomo Halevi Alkabez, who not only composed poems but also the music to accompany them. And whenever he sang the songs he had composed, he held all enthralled. His songs even attracted the birds who flew from all directions to nest in the trees of Safed and listen. And on every Shabbat eve, when the poet sang *L'khah Dodi,* they also joined in harmony. Thus when the Sabbath was welcomed, peace and joy descended upon Safed.

Although the Jews had many Arab friends, the house in which Shlomo Alkabez lived was owned by an Arab who hated the Jews. In this peaceful community, Jews and Arabs mingled commercially and socially. But this Arab landlord plotted evil against the Jews, especially against the poet, of whose golden voice he was envious. He threatened to evict him from his house and burn the table on which Shlomo composed his songs, but he feared the wrath of the other Arabs who loved the sweet singer of Galilee.

One Sabbath eve, as Shlomo and the birds sang together, he heard a shrill voice from behind a round hilltop.

"Stop that noise!"

Though the poet was startled, the birds merely fluttered their wings for a moment and then began again to sing, and Shlomo Alkabez's voice rose even louder and sweeter:

> *L'khah Dodi likrat kalah p'nay Shabbat n'kab'lah.*
> "Come, my Beloved, with chorus of praise,
>   Welcome Bride Sabbath, Queen of the days."

Thus they ushered in the Sabbath Queen as she made her weekly entrance through the hills of Safed.

One dark, starless night, Shlomo was sitting in his candle-lit room when his landlord pounced upon him and drove a knife through his heart.

"Now this screecher will no longer torture me with his songs!" he gloated. "No more shall I have to listen to his weird singing!"

The Arab wiped the blood from the floor, carried the poet's body into the garden, and tossed it into the hole he had dug. Thus no one would know of his crime.

In a short time, Rabbi Lurie, the Rabbi of Safed, and all Shlomo's friends came looking for him, but no one knew where he had gone or why he had vanished. Some thought he might have gone up into the mountains in order to find solitude and compose more poems and songs.

As usual, on the following Sabbath eve, Rabbi Lurie and his followers assembled in the poet's garden to recite the *Kabbalat Shabbat* and greet the Sabbath Queen. They tried to sing, but their tones were hollow and reflected their sadness. Their beloved poet was not with them. Then, abruptly, they heard hundreds of birds singing in the trees all around them.

"See!" said Rabbi Lurie. "The birds know it is not permissible to be sad on the Sabbath; all their songs are songs of joy."

The gathering, as usual, began to sing *L'khah Dodi,* and to their astonishment, the birds sang the same melody.

From then on, the same thing happened every Sabbath eve, and all listeners were enchanted. But the Arab landlord grew more and more viciously offensive.

"Why do you come here?" he shouted. "Your screeching poet is not here. He does not live here any more. This is my garden; I own it. Stay away from here!"

But Rabbi Lurie and his students could not stay away from the garden because they could not sing Shlomo's songs in any other place and neither could the birds.

The assassin was haunted day and night by the thought that the poet's songs were still being sung in his garden.

"I thought I was rid of all this," he moaned, "but it's getting much worse. Every Friday at sundown they keep on coming and singing, and the birds make their usual racket. I've had enough. I'll drive them out for good. I simply won't stand it any longer."

On the following Sabbath eve, just as the sun was setting, he hid behind the trees and waited for Rabbi Lurie and his followers. When they began to chant their welcome to the Sabbath, knife in hand, he dashed out, yelling: "Get out of here, all of you, or I'll kill you!"

He began brandishing his knife and swinging it back and forth when he was suddenly blinded by a cover of wings and deafened by the chirping of hundreds of birds. Dropping the knife in hand, he dashed out, yelling: "Get out of here, all of

"Allah! Allah! A thousand demons are after me! A thousand demons!"

But as soon as he had left, the birds swooped down from the trees and began scratching and digging in the soil.

"What are they looking for?" wondered the worshipers. "How strange! They're not searching for worms and they're not singing their usual songs."

The persistent birds did not stop scratching until they had uncovered the body of a man, and then they flew back into the branches.

"Look! A corpse!" cried one of Rabbi Lurie's students. "A body buried here in Shlomo's garden!" All crowded around, gazing horror-stricken into the shallow grave.

"Shlomo!" they cried out in anguish as they recognized their beloved poet. "Shlomo! Shlomo Alkabez! The Arab killed him and buried him here. That's why he didn't want us in his garden."

They covered the body and, after *Shabbat,* went to the Judge of Safed and explained what had happened. The Judge immediately sent officers of the law to seize the assassin who was hiding in the forest, and the following day he had him executed.

Now we know why *Shabbat Shirah,* the Sabbath on which we remember the birds, is observed the same week as *Tu Bishevat.* Birds and trees! Both help to bring about justice.

ZALMAN'S PURIM GIFT

On one sad Purim during the war, Zalman, a prisoner of war, lay despondent on his bunk. He wanted, as in previous years, to fulfill the *mitzvah* of *mishloah manot,** the sending of gifts and portions to the poor. But here he was, alone and in a strange country. He knew, however, that God was with him, because in his loneliness he repeated day after day the Psalm which brought him the most comfort: *Ki atah imadi* "Thou, O God, art with me" (23:4).

On this Purim day, he turned to God: "O Master of the world, this day I cannot send a Purim gift to the needy, but I would like to send You my *shalah manot*. I have no wine, but I have my tears. Accept them as wine; they are not the juice of grapes but they are the juice of my eyes. I have no cup for my tears, but I have my hands. Therefore I shed tears into my hands which serve as a cup. Please accept these tears as my *shalah manot.*"

Zalman raised his hands full of tears and vowed: "I promise You, O Lord, that when the war ends, if I am still alive, I will send a real *shalah manot* in Your name to the poor and lonely."

The angels carried Zalman's Purim gift to God, placed it on the table of the heavenly *seudah* "feast," and it was the finest *shalah manot* in Paradise. All the angels admired it and asked: "Who sent this *shalah manot?*" God told them: "It was from Zalman, who offered to sacrifice his life that the world might be free."

God was so pleased with this *shalah manot,* that, when the war was over, and all prisoners set free, He decreed that Zalman be the first to set sail for the newly declared State of Israel and, on every Purim thereafter, Zalman brought his *shalah manot* to some family of newly arrived immigrants who were celebrating their first Purim in a free and democratic land.

---

* Commonly known as *"shalah manot."*

EVERY FESTIVAL HAS ITS SOLEMN ASPECT

Every Festival has its joyous and solemn aspect. At the delightful Passover Seder, when Jewish families are reunited and joy prevails, in the midst of their rejoicing they eat *maror* "bitter herbs," thus recalling the bitter sufferings of our ancestors enslaved in Egypt. On Passover, the Jew in his happiness also voices his concern for those whose lives are still embittered and who yearn for freedom.

Sukkot, another joyous holiday, also has its solemn aspect. We leave the comforts of our homes for frail, temporary booths. Though Sukkot is called *z'man simhatenu* "the season of our joy," we personally experience not only the life of those who dwelt in booths on their journey to the Promised Land, but also the life of those who live in primitive *maabarot* (temporary barracks) in Israel and all who dwell in poverty-stricken slums all over the world.

Likewise, the joyful Festival of Purim is saddened by the remembrance of an ancient enemy. On *Shabbat Zakhor* preceding Purim, we read that portion of the Bible which admonishes us to remember Amalek, the treacherous enemy who attacked the weak and unarmed Children of Israel (Deuteronomy 25:17-19). According to tradition, Haman is a descendant of Amalek. And Purim enjoins us constantly to be alert to recognize the dangers of prejudice and hate not only of the Jew but of any people. "Eternal vigilance is the price of liberty." On the day before we celebrate the merry Purim, we observe the Fast of Esther, commemorating that day when Jews in Persia were threatened with extinction.

Even while we feast and drink at the Purim *Seudah,* we recall the persecution of Jews in all countries and all ages. And in addition, we are mindful of those in our own communities who need our help. The holiday is not complete unless we fulfill the *mitzvah* of *mishloah manot,* the sending of gifts to the needy.

PURIM LIKE YOM KIPPURIM

The Talmud tells us that at some future time all Jewish festivals will be annulled, but Purim will remain. Perhaps the reason for this is that Purim is the holiday of joy.

The Kabalists assert that Purim is as important as Yom Kippur. Although there is a striking similarity in the name, Purim and Yom Kippurim, they differ in many respects.

On Purim the Jew occupies himself all day with the reading of the *Megillah*, the Scroll of Esther, with *mishloah manot*, the sending of gifts to friends and needy people, and with the Purim *Seudah* Feast. In contrast, on Yom Kippur the Jew occupies himself all day with prayer, fasting and confession of sins.

On the day before Purim, *Ta'anit Esther*, it is a *mitzvah* to fast, and on Purim it is a *mitzvah* to eat; while on the day before Yom Kippur it is a *mitzvah* to eat and on Yom Kippur it is a *mitzvah* to fast.

Thus, say the Kabalists, there are many ways of serving God: by prayer, repentance and the determination to improve our ways; and also by rejoicing, sending gifts to the needy and participating in family fellowship at the *Seudah*.

The Hasidim like the Kabalists emphasize the joyous aspect of religion and therefore they too contend that Purim is as important as Yom Kippur. They agree with the Psalmist: "Serve the Lord with gladness; come before Him with singing" (Psalm 100:2).

GOD'S NAME OMITTED FROM THE MEGILLAH

It is noteworthy that the name of God does not even once appear in the *Megillah*, the Scroll of Esther, which is read on the Festival of Purim. Several explanations are given for this omission. Some say that, because this holiday is one of revelry and noisemaking, it would be sacrilegious to mention God's name when this Scroll is read.

Others say that when the earlier Books of the Bible were written, the theocentric view prevailed: i.e. everything was expounded from the point of view of God, with the Creator as the pivot of all man's acts. But when the Book of Esther was included in the Bible, the anthropocentric view prevailed: i.e. that man's central role was accentuated. This anthropocentric philosophy did not imply that the people were any less God-minded than before, but that the focus of attention had changed: man and then God instead of God and then man. In our day, the theocentric view is still reflected in our normal conversation as when we say: *im Yirtzeh Hashem* "God willing"; *Barukh Hashem* "Praised be God"; and *Todah l'El* "Thank God."

Another reason has been propounded as to why the name of God is not mentioned in the Book of Esther. The *Sidrah Tetzaveh* (Exodus 27:20-30:10) is read before Purim (with the exception of Leap Year). In that *Sidrah*, the name of Moses does not once appear. The Bible tells us that, when the Children of Israel sinned by worshiping the golden calf and God wanted to destroy them, Moses pleaded with God: "Blot out my name if You will not forgive my people." Legend tells us that Moses really meant that it was not important that his name appear as long as God would forgive his people. For that reason, God forgave the people for Moses's sake and omitted Moses's name from this *Sidrah*.

In the days of Esther and Mordecai, the legend continues, the people were resentful that God had omitted the name of Moses from the *Sidrah* which is read before Purim.

"It is unfair," they complained. "Moses made great sacrifices for his people and, because God omitted his name from this *Sidrah Tetzaveh*, we will protest by omitting God's name from the Book of Esther. At all times should a leader be recognized and appreciated," they said.

REDEMPTION THROUGH LOVE

Before the traditional Jew observes the Festival of Passover, he contributes to *Maot Hitim* "money for wheat," a fund to provide Passover food for the needy. This fund is also called *Kimha d'Pesha* "flour for Passover." Why is there such a fund only for Passover and not for Sukkot and Shavuot? Are there not just as many needy people when we celebrate the other Pilgrimage Festivals? Why only on Passover do we open the door at the Seder and say: *Kol dikhfin yetay v'yekhul* "Let all who are hungry come and eat?" Why do we not extend a similar invitation on Sukkot and Shavuot?

According to tradition, the Temple was destroyed and the Jews lost their independence because of *sinat hinam* "causeless hatred" and their redemption will come through *ahavah* "lovingkindness." We are to help the needy on all Festivals, but especially on Passover which recalls the liberation of the Jews from their difficult and impoverished existence as slaves in Egypt. On Passover especially, the Jew was to set an example of helpfulness and hospitality to others, because we are told that the final redemption of the Jews and all humanity will take place on Passover.

THE MIDDLE MATZAH

Passover is called *Hag Hamatzot,* the Festival of Unleavened Bread. At the Seder table, three *matzot* are provided for the ritual ceremony. The middle *matzah* is divided in two: one half is broken into small pieces and distributed to all present for the *motzi* prayer at the beginning of the meal; the other half is set aside for the *afikoman,* symbol of the paschal lamb to be eaten at the conclusion of the meal. The middle *matzah* thus has great significance in the Seder ritual.

But the middle *matzah* also has a deeper meaning because it has something in common with the name of the Festival, *Hag Hamatzot. Matzot* is spelled *mem tzadik tav* (Exodus 12:18). The letters *mem* and *tav* form the word *met* "a corpse." But the middle letter *tzadik* suggests justice and kindness. When the Children of Israel worshiped idols in Egypt, they sank so low that they were like a *met*—dead. But when Moses came and taught them justice, kindness and love, God redeemed them. The *tzadik* entered their lives, and the *met* became *matzot.* Then came *Hag Hamatzot,* the Festival of Freedom.

When we are not kind and just, we are like a *met* "a corpse," but when these virtues enter our lives we are truly alive and free. The *tzadik* is in the *middle* of the word *matzot* and by association of ideas, the middle *matzah* on the Seder table thus assumes added significance.

THE UNIVERSAL CHARACTER OF PASSOVER

All Jewish Festivals have a universal message, as is demonstrated by the three Pilgrimage Festivals. Sukkot, called *Hag Heh-asif,* the Feast of Ingathering, is the forerunner of the American Thanksgiving, and the *Sukkah* (Tabernacle or Booth) is the symbol of peace.

Shavuot commemorates the giving of the Ten Commandments on Mount Sinai, and these commandments were intended for all peoples. The Midrash tells us that the Ten Commandments were proclaimed in the seventy then known languages of mankind, so that all might know and observe them.

The universal note is especially stressed on Passover. The command: "You shall rejoice," which occurs three times in connection with the Festival of Sukkot (Leviticus 23:40; Deuteronomy 16:14,15) is omitted when the Bible speaks of Passover. Why is this? Passover is supposed to be the happiest holiday because it recalls the end of slavery and the birth of freedom. Why should not the Children of Israel be as happy on Passover as they were commanded to be on Sukkot?

The Midrash relates that, when the Egyptians were drowning in the Red Sea and the angels wanted to sing "Halleluyah!" God rebuked them:

"How can you sing Halleluyah when My children are drowning?" (*Megillah 10 b*).

For this reason, only half of the *Hallel* and not the complete *Hallel* (Psalms 113-118) is recited during the last six days of Passover. In God's sight, all people are His children and all nations His creation.

"Have we not all one Father? Has not one God created us all? Why do we deal treacherously, man against his brother . . . ?" (Malachi 2:10).

"Are you not like the Ethiopians to Me, O Children of Israel? says the Lord" (Amos 9:7).

For the same reason, at the Seder we pour off ten drops of wine from our second cup as we enumerate the ten plagues.

The Psalmist tells us: "Wine gladdens the heart of man," but how can the heart be fully glad when we know that Israel's redemption brought suffering to the Egyptians? We cannot be happy when any human being, however much an enemy he may be, suffers persecution or tyranny.

Hence, at the Seder, our second cup of wine must never be full. The measure of our gladness is to be purposely diminished; therefore the command: "You shall be altogether joyous," is not mentioned in connection with Passover. This may also be the reason why in The Song of Moses (Exodus 15:1-18), the verb is in the future and not in the past. We read *Az yashir Moshe* "Then Moses *will* sing," not *Az shar Moshe* "Then Moses *sang*" to indicate that the Exodus was only the beginning of redemption and that redemption can only be complete when mankind learns to live together in peace.

Both the custom of reciting only half *Hallel* and of pouring off some of the wine as an expression of sympathy to the Egyptians, emphasizes the admonition: "Do not rejoice when your enemy falls" (Proverbs 24:17).

There is a Talmudic legend which tells us that Pharaoh was not drowned with his people. In the daily prayer before the *Amidah,* in recounting the crossing of the Red Sea, we read: *Ehad mehem lo notar* "Not one of them remained." The Hasidim analyzed each word of this Hebrew idiomatic expression to justify this legend. They say: *Ehad mehem* "One of them," —Pharaoh, who ten times said *lo* "no" to Moses's plea "Let my people go!" *notar* "he remained." Why was Pharaoh spared? Because Moses had shown him the error of his ways and Pharaoh thereafter repented and became a friend of the Children of Israel. We read in *Avot de Rav Natan: Aizehu gibor, mi she'oseh sono ohavo* "Who is a hero? He who converts an enemy into a friend." Moses was a hero because he turned his enemy into a friend.

HAD GADYAH

The closing hymn of the Seder, *Had Gadyah* "One Kid," has been variously interpreted. Rabbi Jonathan Eybeschutz and others have interpreted it as a hymn of God's providence. God is forever manifest in the history of mankind. Israel, "the kid," redeemed by God from Egypt through Moses and Aaron (the two zuzim), succumbs to a mightier empire, which in turn is defeated by other empires, and so on, until God's rule of justice shall triumph.

The cat in this hymn is interpreted as Assyria; the dog, Babylonia; the stick, Persia; the water, Greece; the ox, Rome; the slaughterer, the Moslems; the angel of death, the European nations. But the Holy One of Israel will finally stamp out all tyranny, deliver all His children from oppression, re-establish the principle of justice, and inaugurate the age of peace among all nations. The Seder, symbolizing humanity's love of freedom, thus ends on a hopeful and joyous note.

There is another interpretation: the two *zuzim* (coins) refer to Moses and David, both shepherds. Why was Moses chosen to be the leader of the Children of Israel? When God saw Moses was so kind that he carried a tired lamb in his arms, He made him the shepherd and leader of His people.

David was likewise chosen to be King because he too was a kind shepherd. He separated the younger from the older sheep when the weaker were unable to keep pace with the stronger. David loved his flock and played melodies for them on his flute: one to summon them to pasture; another to entertain them; a third to gather them together and bring them back to the fold.

In the *kriat shema,* the prayer before going to bed, Moses is said to be at the right of the angel Michael; and David at the left of the angel Gabriel.

Moses gave us the Torah; David, the State; and both are essential for the preservation of the Jewish people and the development of their spiritual heritage.

THE SONG OF FREEDOM

On the Seventh Day of Passover, when the Torah Reading deals with the miracle of the Crossing of the Red Sea, hundreds of Jews in Israel go down to the sea at night and there chant The Song of Moses (Exodus 15:1-18).

This comparatively new custom is becoming more and more popular. Why is this? The Israelis go down to the sea not only to commemorate an ancient miracle but also a modern miracle. Like their ancestors who were emancipated from Egyptian oppression, these Israelis in modern times have been liberated from enemies who surrounded them on all sides, and many have experienced the ghastly horrors of concentration camps. Their liberation was indeed like the miracle when the Red Sea was divided. They certainly understand why the Bible does not say *Az shar Moshe* "Then Moses *sang*," but *Az yashir Moshe* "Then Moses *will* sing."

Liberation did not end with the crossing of the Red Sea. That was just the beginning. When all who are now enslaved or suffer tyranny shall be set free, like Moses they *will* sing their song of praise to their Redeemer.

A NEW PARTNER FOR THE SEVENTH DAY
OF PASSOVER

The Song of Moses *Az yashir* (Exodus 15:1-18) is the Torah portion for the Seventh Day of Passover. The mystics tell us that the Seventh Day of Passover complained to the angels: "Every day of Passover has a partner except me. The partner of the First Day is *Tishah B'Av*. The partner of the Second Day is *Shavuot*. The partner of the Third Day is *Rosh Hashanah*. The partner of the Fourth is *Kriat HaTorah* (*Simhat Torah*). The partner of the Fifth is *Tzom* (*Yom Kippur*). The partner of the Sixth Day is *Purim*. Why is it that I, the Seventh Day, have no partner?" *

The angels replied: "Ah, yes, in the future you too shall have a partner and it will be *Yom Haatzma-ut*."

And so it came to pass. In 1948, when the State of Israel was established, a new holiday came into being on the Fifth Day of the month of *Iyar* which, according to the Hebrew calendar, occurs on the same day of the week as the Seventh Day of Passover. The Seventh Day of Passover at last has a partner, *Yom Haatzma-ut*, the State of Israel's Independence Day!

It is also noteworthy that the holidays which are the partners of the Days of Passover, beginning with *Tishah B'Av*, commence with Hebrew letters in the reverse order of the alphabet and that the last one, *Atzma-ut*, begins with the letter *ayin* which, in reverse order, follows the letter *peh* in Purim, the holiday which is the partner of the Sixth Day of Passover. What a remarkable coincidence!

---

* To understand the question raised by the Seventh Day, it should be noted that according to the Hebrew calendar, the First Day of Passover occurs on the same day of the week as does *Tishah B'Av;* the Second Day of Passover occurs on the same day as *Shavuot;* and the schedule of the other days of Passover is as indicated above.

THE PARABLE OF GOD'S LOVE

During the Festival of Passover, Solomon's *Song of Songs* is read in the Synagogue. Various explanations for this have been offered. One is, that Solomon sings of spring and romance, both appropriate to this Festival.

> "Rise up, my love, my fair one and come away.
> For lo the winter is past, the rain is over and gone;
> The flowers appear on the earth;
> The time of singing is come . . ." (2:10-12).

The Midrash tells us that, as a young man, King Solomon composed *The Song of Songs* as a Canticle devoted to romance and beauty. In middle age, he wrote *Proverbs* which abounds in wisdom, profound truths and sage admonition. When he was old, he wrote *Ecclesiastes,* depicting the pessimistic and tragic aspects of life as summarized in the refrain: "Vanity of vanities, all is vanity."

These changes of mood are exemplified in the lives of most human beings. When they are young, they are full of romance, hope and idealism. When they reach middle age, they are realistic, experienced, and can offer sound advice to others. When they are old, they become feeble and cynical. The same is true of nations; though Israel is an ancient nation, Israel is an exception and is revealing all the vigor, vitality and enthusiasm of youth.

The brief eight chapters of *The Songs of Songs* have often puzzled scholars. Some maintain that they are love poems from a bridegroom to his bride. Others contend that the Book consists of fragments of a love drama: Shulamit, a beautiful maiden, is betrothed to a handsome shepherd. The King's counselor saw her and was so impressed with her beauty that, in the hope that the King would win her love and ask her to become his wife, carried her off to the palace. But Shulamit spurns the luxuries of the palace and rejects the advances of the King. Finally, she is reunited with her shepherd lover to whom she was ever faithful.

Whichever view one accepts, the question remains: why is such a romantic Book included in the Bible? Why did the great sage, Rabbi Akiba, exclaim: "The world was never so fortunate as when this Book became part of the Bible." The accepted interpretation is that *The Song of Songs* is not to be taken literally but as a parable illustrating God's love for Israel. Israel, the Bride, has been tempted by other nations to renounce her religion and her Torah for a life of materialism and luxury, but she remains forever true to her one love, the Lord God.

Some of the mystics carry the parable still further. The dispersion of the Jews is explained as a lovers' quarrel. God was angry because Israel had sinned, and therefore He and Israel were separated. Both desired a reconciliation, but each was waiting for the other to take the first step. Now after centuries of estrangement, God took the first step toward a reconciliation by establishing the State of Israel.

"Fear not," He said, "for I am with you.
 I will bring your seed from the east,
 And gather you from the west;
 I will say to the north: 'Give up!'
 And to the south: 'Do not withhold!
 Bring my sons from afar,
 And my daughters from the end of the earth' " (Isaiah 43:5,6).

And Israel replied in the words of *The Song of Songs:* "My Beloved is mine and I am His" (2:16).

The reconciliation will be complete when Israel shall not only build homes, factories and cities, and be materially self-sufficient, but shall also be spiritually strong to fulfill the prophecies of Isaiah: "Zion will be redeemed through justice," and "Out of Zion shall go forth the Torah and the word of God from Jerusalem" (Isaiah 1:27; 2:3).

Other Comments on Passover

THE CHAMBER OF DESTRUCTION
AND DAVID'S TOMB

On Mount Zion there are two memorials closely associated in space, time and philosophic significance: *Martef Hashoah* "The Chamber of Destruction," and *Kever David* "The Tomb of David." One symbolizes the past sufferings of the Jewish people; the other, their future redemption. In the Chamber of Destruction are the urns containing the ashes of many who perished in Nazi ovens, and there are also ghastly visible reminders of the Nazis' inhuman savagery perpetrated against innocent and defenseless people. Above the Chamber is David's Tomb, reminiscent of Israel's ancient glory and its future promise.

The Tomb and the Chamber are closely associated not only in their position but also in time. The 27th day of the month of *Nisan,* the Memorial Day for six million Jews, is called *Yom Hashoah* "The Day of Destruction" and *Yom HaKaddish* "The Day of Reciting the Kaddish Prayer" (for the Six Million). In order to fittingly observe this sad Memorial Day, many assemble in the Chamber of Destruction. A week later, however, on the 5th day of the month of *Iyar,* Israel's Independence Day, many gather to observe that joyous day at David's Tomb.

In Jewish philosophy, these two observances are closely related. There are *Meshiah* and *hevli Meshiah* "the Messiah and the sufferings before the coming of the Messiah." The Rabbis describe the bitter sufferings that must precede the coming of the Messiah. In nature, the sky is darkest before dawn. The bird, symbol of freedom, does not see the light until the egg is broken. From the ashes of destruction emerged the State of Israel. The suffering and destruction of the six million must not be in vain. We have faith that redemption will soon come, not only for the Jews, but for all mankind.

THE BERGEN-BELSEN SHOFAR

The Midrash tells us that every part of the ram which was sacrificed in place of Isaac was later put to constructive use. Out of its ashes, the altar of the Temple was erected; from the sinews were made the strings of King David's harp; from the skin was fashioned the belt of the Prophet Elijah. One of the horns became the Shofar that was sounded on Mount Sinai when the Torah was given. The other horn was preserved for the Shofar which is to herald the beginning of Israel's redemption.

On Israel's Independence Day a Shofar is sounded. On Mount Zion, the Shofar sounded is the very one which was used in the concentration camp of Bergen-Belsen. Why is this particular Shofar used? At Bergen-Belsen, despite the prohibition against conducting any religious service, amidst the terrific din of sirens and machine-gun fire, a Shofar was sounded on Rosh Hashanah. At the close of Yom Kippur, when it was again blown, it sent forth piercing sounds of bullets and machine-guns. The worshipers were startled and could only explain this by suspecting that the Shofar had that day become defective and had absorbed the noise of sirens and shrapnel. Thereafter, mysteriously, each time the Bergen-Belsen Shofar is used, the sound of machine-gun fire is heard. These bring back memories of the tragic fate of six million Jews, upon whose ashes, according to the mystics, the new State of Israel has been built. That is the reason for the sounding of this particular Shofar. The Shofar of Bergen-Belsen is said to announce *athalta di-g'ulah* "the beginning of redemption." It is believed that this Shofar will ultimately herald the redemption of Israel and all mankind.

THE LEGEND OF THE FLOWER

The Kabalists refer to the final redemption of Israel as *perah* "a flower." God, they say, will bring about this redemption through His mystical Name consisting of seventy-two letters and will gather the exiles from the four corners of the earth. Four times seventy-two is 288. The numerical value of the letters *peh resh het* of the Hebrew word for "flower" is also 288; therefore the Kabalists refer to the Redemption as a "flowering."

Our Rabbis maintained that the Land of Israel would bloom like a flower only through the efforts of the Children of Israel. Without its people, Nahmonides taught, the land will not blossom and flourish.

The Curator of Mount Zion instituted the custom of presenting a pressed flower to every pilgrim who ascended the Holy Mountain. When asked why he does not give a fresh flower, he related a story, several variations of which are extant. It is believed that the original version goes back to the period when the Crusaders were conquering Jerusalem.

When the Prince of Coucy was about to join the Crusaders on their way to wrest the Holy Land from the Moslems, he came to bid farewell to his friend, the Rabbi of Coucy. The Prince asked the Rabbi what he would like him to bring back from Jerusalem.

"My friend," said the Rabbi, "please bring me some sign of life to comfort me in the knowledge that Jerusalem has not been left barren; a sign of vitality that will bolster my faith in the eventual regeneration of the Holy City and the return of my people now dispersed throughout the world."

The Prince promised to fulfill the Rabbi's request, and departed. Several years went by and finally the Prince of Coucy returned home. The Prince called on the Rabbi and handed him the promised gift. It was a wilted flower.

"In all of Jerusalem, I could not find anything with a spark of life in it," explained the Prince. "The city has been ploughed up; it is completely desolate and in ruins. On Mount Zion, I found this wilted flower. I tried to revive it with water but to no avail. It is the only thing I could find that had any life."

As the Rabbi took the withered flower into his trembling hands and pressed it to his lips, tears rolled down his cheeks. As soon as the tears touched the flower, miraculously, the petals opened and the flower blossomed out.

Amazed, the Prince's eyes widened, but after a moment, the significance of this startling phenomenon dawned on him.

"You have brought the flower back to life," he said. "I see now that dried and desolate, Zion awaits the return of her sons, because only through their efforts will she blossom and live."

When the Curator concluded his story he explained: "That is why those ascending Mount Zion receive a pressed flower to impress upon them that there are still areas of desolation in Israel." And he tells the pilgrims: "Through your efforts combined with ours, all the desolate areas will one day blossom and flourish."

WEDDINGS ON LAG BA'OMER

In ancient times, on the second day of Passover, our ancestors brought into the Temple at Jerusalem an *omer* "a measure" of their first barley harvest. In accordance with the Biblical command, at the end of forty-nine days from that date, the Festival of Shavuot was to be celebrated (Leviticus 23:10,15,16; Deuteronomy 16:9). The practice of counting forty-nine days, called *Sefirah* "counting" is still observed.

During *Sefirah,* among Orthodox and Conservative Jews, there are certain restrictions regarding marriages, but on *Lag Ba'Omer,* the thirty-third day of the *omer,* weddings are permissible. Several reasons are given for this. One is that the persecutions of the Jews which occurred during *Sefirah* came to an end on *Lag Ba'Omer.* Another is that a plague which had broken out during this period was arrested on that day.

There is a midrash that a couple once came to Rabbi Shimon ben Yohai, the mystic of Meron, and requested a divorce.

"Why do you want a divorce?" asked the Rabbi. "Are you unhappy?"

"No. We love each other," said the husband, "but we have been childless for ten years."

"Very well," said the Rabbi. "You began your marriage with a *seudah* 'a feast.' You should end it with a *seudah.*"

The husband agreed, and at the feast, everyone was cheerful and toasted one *l'hayim* "To life!" after another. The husband, after paying tribute to his wife, said to her: "As a token of our love these ten years, you may take from this house anything you most desire."

After the meal and several more drinks, the husband fell asleep, and the wife asked her friends to carry him to the home of her parents. When he awoke the following morning, he was surprised to find himself in another house.

"Where am I?" he asked. "What am I doing here?"

And the wife replied: "Didn't you say that I could take with me from our home whatever I like best? Well, I like you best of all, and so I had you brought here."

The husband was so deeply touched by his wife's affection that he decided to forget all about the divorce.

Rabbi Shimon ben Yohai always found great joy in uniting and reconciling estranged couples. When he died on *Lag Ba'-Omer,* the people determined to commemorate the life and good deeds of this man who had brought happiness to so many families. What better way is there to perpetuate his memory, they decided, than by permitting weddings to take place on *Lag Ba'Omer.*

THE LIGHT THAT SAVES THE WORLD

Lag Ba'Omer commemorates the *yahrzeit* of a great mystic, Rabbi Shimon ben Yohai. According to Kabalistic lore, we learn that as long as this sage lived, the rainbow which reminded man of God's protection did not appear in the sky because the brilliance of this saintly scholar's mind protected the world against all destructive floods.

A strange remark is attributed to Shimon ben Yohai: "Together with the light of Jotham, son of Uzziah, I can protect the world from the beginning to the end of time."

At first glance it would appear that this scholar was boastful, arrogant and vain. On the contrary, he was humble and devout. Then what is the meaning of this mystifying utterance? What was the merit of Jotham that he deserved such praise? Though his father became a leper and was not able to continue reigning as King, Jotham nevertheless so honored his father that he issued all decrees and did everything in the name of his father as though Uzziah actually ruled. His love and respect for his father, his scrupulous observance of the Fifth Commandment: "Honor your father and mother," made him, according to the Kabalists, worthy to be considered mankind's eternal protector. In the blaze of such light, humanity could be spared destruction.

Where there is respect and love for parents, family life is wholesome and the nation is secure.

THE RAINBOW A SYMBOL IN ISRAEL

Lag Ba'Omer commemorates not only the *yahrzeit* of Shimon
ben Yohai, the renowned mystic of Meron, but also the rebellion
of Bar Kokhba against the Romans in 135 C. E. On this Festival
of *Lag Ba'Omer,* tens of thousands of Jews, oriental and occi-
dental, gather in Meron, Israel, where, in the forest, children
shoot arrows from their bows. Hence, the *keshet* "the bow,"
is associated with *Lag Ba'Omer.*

The *keshet* also means "the rainbow." The rainbow which
flashes across the sky in one unified arch consisting of many
colors all blending together is a symbol of unity and brother-
hod. Thus the *keshet* "the bow" symbolizing war, but also
unity, is associated with the life of Shimon ben Yohai.

In Noah's time there was a lack of unity among men. Every
man was for himself and each was against his neighbor; therefore a flood was sent to inundate the earth. When we look up
and behold the rainbow so glorious in its many colors, we learn
from it that people of all colors and beliefs may harmoniously
live together in unity as brothers.

The mystics say that in the days of Shimon ben Yohai, no
rainbow was ever seen because the spiritual essence of the rainbow was on earth in his person and he united all people. In his
day, all those who had food shared it with those who had none,
and those who had garments gave part of them to the unfor-
tunates who had no clothing. Thus in Rabbi Shimon ben
Yohai's lifetime, the spirit of solidarity and brotherhood was
everywhere felt and expressed.

The same is happening today. *Kibbutz Galiyot* "The ingathering of immigrants from the nations of the world," is symbolized by the *keshet* "the bow" of Shimon ben Yohai. Like the
rainbow, Jews of all types and ethnic origins are today united
to help one another and live harmoniously in their new homeland.

THE CRACK IN THE UPPER LINTEL

On *Lag Ba'Omer,* thousands make a pilgrimage to Meron and offer prayers in the old Synagogue called by Shimon ben Yohai's name.

This old Synagogue was recently rebuilt. But when the workers were about to restore its gate, the mystics asked them to leave it alone because they believe that when it is time for the *mashkef* "the upper lintel" to fall down, the Messiah will come to redeem the Children of Israel. If the beam over the gate were restored, the coming of the Messiah would be delayed; therefore the gate was left untouched.

In the War of Independence, when the Israelis took Meron, the elders heard a crashing sound. The *mashkef* began to fall, but it did not drop to the ground; and the crack in the stone can still be seen.

How symbolic is this of the redemption taking place in our day! The deliverance has begun but is not yet complete. It will not be complete the mystics of Meron say, until the people fill their lives with the performance of good deeds. Then the *mashkef* will fall and at long last the Messiah will come and bring deliverance and freedom to all who are homeless and oppressed.

SHAVUOT IS THE SOURCE

There is a legend that the Festival of Shavuot once complained to God: "Every *Yom Tov* (holiday) has its special *mitzvah*. Passover has *matzot* (unleavened bread); Sukkot, the *etrog* (citron), *lulav* (palm branch), and the *Sukkah* (booth); Hanukkah has the eight candles; Purim has the *megillah* (Scroll of Esther). I alone have no special *mitzvah*."

"You do not require a special *mitzvah*," God replied. "You are the source of all the *mitzvot* because your holiday commemorates not only the Giving of the Ten Commandments but also, according to tradition, the entire Torah with all the *mitzvot*."

Shavuot was still not satisfied. It said: "Every holiday has its own particular volume of the Talmud: *Rosh Hashannah, Yoma* (Yom Kippur), *Pesahim, Sukkah,* and *Megillah*. But there is no volume of the Talmud for me." *

"You don't need a special volume," God replied. "Every volume of Talmud comes from you. You are the source of all Jewish learning. To make certain that people remember this, I have initiated the tradition of *Tikun Shavuot* (an arrangement of texts for Shavuot) which the people will read on the first night of your Festival. This *Tikun* consists of the beginning and conclusion of every *Sidrah* (Weekly Torah Reading), of every Biblical Book and of every Tractate of the Mishnah."

---

* The *Talmud Shevuot*, similar in sound to Shavuot, deals with the subject of oaths and not with the Festival of Shavuot.

THE TEN COMMANDMENTS

Tradition tells us that when God revealed Himself on Mount Sinai and gave the Commandments to the Children of Israel, all the people praised the Lord in the words of the Psalmist: "I will extol Thee with my whole heart . . . I will worship in Thy holy Temple and praise Thy name for Thy lovingkindness and for Thy truth; . . . All the kings of the earth shall praise Thee for they have heard the words of Thy mouth" (Psalm 138:1,2,4).

Why is *imray pikha* "the words of Thy mouth," expressed in the plural and not in the singular? The entire Torah is called the *word* of God, not the *words* of God.

According to Hasidic lore, we are told that when God began to proclaim the Ten Commandments and the people heard the words: "*I* am the Lord, your God . . . You shall have no other gods before *Me* . . . You shall not take *My* name in vain . . . ," they were disappointed.

They said: *Likhvod atzmo Hu doresh* "Only for His own honor does He speak." But when God continued: "Honor your father and your mother . . . You shall not kill . . . You shall not steal . . ." the people exclaimed: "Ah, God speaks not only for Himself, but is interested in *our* welfare." Then they began to adore and praise Him. For that reason, the plural is used in the phrase, "the words of Thy mouth" (*Yalkut Shimoni* on Psalm 138).

THE MORAL LAW

According to the Talmud, the tablets on which the Ten Commandments were engraved were prepared on the eve of Creation so that they actually antedate humanity and are therefore independent of time, place or culture. The mystics believe that these tablets were hewn from the sapphire Throne of Glory. The Commandments, given in a desert which belonged exclusively to no one nation, were heard not by the Children of Israel alone, but by the inhabitants of all the earth. The Divine Voice spoke simultaneously in the then known seventy languages so that all could understand. Even the souls of all the unborn generations were assembled at the foot of Mount Sinai.

Our sages held that the sixth day of the month of *Sivan,* commemorating the Giving of the Ten Commandments, is as momentous as the day of Creation. For without the moral law, the creation of the universe would be incomplete. All nations, if they are to endure, must be founded on the principles enunciated in the Ten Commandments.

There are those who maintain that other peoples, preceding the Children of Israel, also proclaimed similar teachings. That may be true. What makes the Ten Commandments of the Bible unique is that they have the Divine stamp on them: "I am the Lord your God."

EVERY MITZVAH IS LIKE A FLOWER

Meir, an aged Jew, too feeble to travel, asked a friend who was about to make a pilgrimage to Jerusalem, to bring him back something that shows the growth and vitality of the Holy Land. Before returning, his friend plucked a beautiful flower but alas, it soon withered. When he brought Meir the flower, he apologized for bringing him a wilted one. But Meir was so happy to see something that came from the Holy Land, that he took the flower in his trembling hands and pressed it to his heart. As he held it close and praised God,—lo and behold!—miraculously, its petals lifted and it began to show life.

Every *mitzvah* is like a flower. If one performs a *mitzvah* perfunctorily, without *kavanah,* feeling, sincerity and enthusiasm, it is like a withered flower, without life and meaning.

We alone can give vitality to a *mitzvah*. Through our fervor and devotion, the *mitzvah* becomes a flower of God which blooms in our garden of meritorious deeds.

To emphasize that a *mitzvah* is like a flower, Sephardic Jews on Shavuot, decorate the *Sefer Torah* with flowers. Ashkenazic Jews adorn the pulpit with flowers and greens.

Other Comments on Shavuot